SECOND CHANCES

More Tales of Found Dogs

Elise Lufkin

Photographs by
Diana Walker

Foreword by
JAMIE LEE CURTIS

THE LYONS PRESS
Guilford, Connecticut
An imprint of The Globe Pequot Press

The Lyons Press is an imprint of The Globe Pequot Press
10 9 8 7 6 5 4 3 2
Printed in China
Book Design by Peter Holm, Sterling Hill Productions
ISBN 1-59228-747-6 (paperback)

The Library of Congress has previously cataloged an earlier (hardcover)
edition as follows:
Lufkin, Elise.
  Second chances: more tales of found dogs / Elise Lufkin;
photographs by Diana Walker; foreword by Jamie Lee Curtis.
    p. cm.
  ISBN 1-59228-140-0 (HC: alk. paper)
  1. Dogs—United States—Anecdotes. 2. Dog adoption—United States
Anecdotes. I. Title.
  SF426.2.L84 2003
  636. 7'0887—dc22
                                    2003017069

To Elise, Margaret, Alison, and Abigail—you inspire me to try to make a difference.

E. B. L

In appreciation of my parents, Dorcas and La, who introduced me to a life full of cats and dogs, making this book truly a labor of love.

D. H. W.

CONTENTS

ACKNOWLEDGMENTS

I am grateful to Lilly Golden at The Lyons Press for her belief in this project and for her help in making it a reality. Other people as well have given me encouragement and significant help in different ways. I would like to thank Colleen Daly, who is truly the godmother of this book, Randi Murray and Amy Rennert of the Amy Rennert Agency, Jamie Lee Curtis, Fran Jewell, Kevin Kendrick, Sue Lavoie, Laurie Leman, Linda Hackett and Russell Munson, Annette and Oscar de la Renta, Barbara-Anne Savino, and especially Diana Walker, for her moving and evocative photographs. For printing the photographs, Diana and I would like to thank Black and White Photo Lab of Arlington, Virginia, and particularly Kit Putnam and April Sauerwine for their help and enthusiasm.

Finally, for the stories in this book as well as those precluded by lack of space, I would like to thank all the generous people who were willing to tell me about their rescued dogs. This book really belongs to them.

AUTHOR'S NOTE: All royalties from this book will be donated to animal-related organizations: various animal shelters, the Great American Mutt Show, and the Delta Society.

MAN'S BEST FRIEND?

I've always considered the old adage about dogs being man's best friend as rather unbalanced. The *American Heritage Dictionary* describes a *friend* as "someone whom one knows, likes, and trusts."

In the media we are saturated with images of men and women, boys and girls, clapping their hands and dropping to their knees as a trusty canine with wagging tail comes bounding over to lick and love the human "friend." The media rarely focuses on the fact that many pets receive little or no attention and, instead, are often taken advantage of, kept around only because they provide constant love and then discarded (or worse) if they become inconvenient or if the human gets bored.

For me, friendship is a two-way street. It's about mutual love and genuine, reciprocal affection. It's about respect and a willingness to help each other, look out for each other. Why is it then that there are so many abandoned, abused, and mistreated dogs? This question cannot be answered by any person who has bonded with a found dog. To us it's simply inconceivable that anyone could fail to cherish these incredible animal friends.

I have known the deep love of three found dogs. None of them was able to tell me the sad story of his previous situation, but Teddy—my dear, departed friend Rick's Lhasa apso—helped me to understand the tragic circumstances surrounding the last year of Rick's too-brief life.

There is an unspoken understanding between a found dog and her human friend. It is a gentle awareness and a quiet acknowledgment of the sadness that filled them, and might have continued to underline both their lives had they not found each other. If you have a friend lucky enough to know a found dog, or have been found by one yourself, you no doubt recognize that certain, special look—a silent, shared language of love and mutual respect and gratitude.

Diana Walker and Elise Lufkin know that look well, and they are devoted to chronicling these extraordinary relationships. In this second volume about found dogs they bring alive more delightful tales of strays and the people who found them. Enjoy their stories, and then go hug your own dogs. Or, dare I say it, take the initiative to go out and open your heart and invite a found dog into your home. It just might be the most important friendship of that dog's life. And yours.

And remember, a best friend is a friend for life.

JAMIE LEE CURTIS

INTRODUCTION

Throughout my life I have been involved with animals—dogs, cats, horses, even snakes. I can't remember a time in my life without a dog. The Christmas card my parents sent the year I was born is a photograph of a plump, smiling baby trying to pull herself up on a large and very patient dog. When I was ten, a small terrier mix turned up at our house and captivated me and my five siblings in about five minutes. She then set out to charm my parents, a more difficult challenge that took the better part of a day. Sweetie Pie stayed with us for fifteen years. Dogs shared the exuberance and fun of my childhood and comforted me through bouts of painful shyness. Fortunately, there was always a dog for solace.

Diana Walker, photographer and creator of the images in this book, has also shared her life with dogs and understands their capacity to enhance our existence. Diana's life has always included dogs; one of her earliest memories is of the family Norwich terrier, Strawberry, giving birth to a litter of puppies in the basement. She now has a loving Labrador shadow named Gus. Diana is quick to point out that her love for dogs has in no way smothered, or even affected, her passion for cats, fifty years of cats—Abdul, Daisy, Fred, and now, only Ginger.

Dogs have enriched my life immeasurably. Working with them has taught me a great deal. Some years ago I initiated a program at my local animal shelter in which volunteers work with dogs to help socialize them. The dogs receive some basic obedience training to make them more attractive as candidates for adoption and more successful in their new homes. Through this work I saw in a concrete way the tragedy of pet overpopulation, and I began to realize how many dogs with real potential are languishing in animal shelters all around the country. I was horrified to learn how many dogs must be killed every year to make room for the next batch of unwanted animals.

Partly in reaction to this bleak side of the work, I began to focus on the happy endings, the success stories. I have always been interested in the bond between people and dogs. Shelter work showed me the special relationship that often blossoms when an animal is rescued. Truly, one man's trash can be another man's treasure.

In 1997 I published *Found Dogs: Tales of Strays Who Landed on Their Feet* to encourage people to consider adopting a homeless dog. I hoped that these stories would lead readers to visit their local shelter instead of the pet shop at the mall. Often puppies in pet stores come from factory farms that produce puppies as a cash crop. In many cases, the dogs—brood bitches, stud dogs, and puppies—are kept in tiny, filthy cages under horrible conditions. Many are diseased; many have serious genetic flaws. According to Roger Caras, a previous executive director of the American Society for the Prevention of Cruelty to Animals, when puppies from these wholesale breeders are delivered to pet stores, "They give them a bath, blow dry and fluff them up, and pray they don't die before they're sold." Purchasing pet-shop puppies only promotes the horrors of puppy mills.

Found Dogs was more successful than I ever imagined it could be. Book sales were much higher than the publisher expected, but for me the best part was meeting so many kindred spirits all over the country, both in person and through letters and e-mail. I met people who are truly awe inspiring in their kindness and generosity, people who have given me a renewed faith in human nature. I met people who have rescued dogs in shelters and dogs surviving on the street. In bookstores, at dog parks and on airplanes I met people who spend much of their time working to find homes for needy animals. Everywhere I heard, "I love *Found Dogs*—it made me laugh and it made me cry—but wait until you hear *my* story!" The sequel, *Second Chances*, was off and running.

I dedicated *Found Dogs* to the matchmakers, people who work to place homeless animals—professionals at shelters as well as individuals with their networks of friends and neighbors. I have tremendous admiration for them and for the work they do. I donate all profits from *Found Dogs* to animal welfare organizations and to shelters large and small. I plan to do the same with *Second Chances*.

To old friends and new ones, I hope that you enjoy this new book. I hope, too, that some of you will think about a dog out there somewhere, a dog who needs you. As Peter Mayle points out in the introduction to *Found Dogs*, "When you adopt a dog, the whole experience is fraught with delightful unpredictability. Very little is certain—except, of course, that you will be giving him a better life. And he will be doing the same for you."

SECOND
CHANCES

CIAO-CIAO AND FRIENDS

—— Leslie Priggen, Animal portrait painter ——

I grew up in England in a house where you could find a dog on almost every chair. I have maintained that tradition. Since I moved up to the country from New York City with five dogs, the population has increased. At one point twelve seemed to be my cruising speed. I wouldn't have it any other way.

Of the original five, only ancient Jamie and Brindle are still with me. Mole, the sweet old black dog, was the first dog I found here. On a bitter cold day in late November I saw her trotting down the middle of the road, dodging cars, or rather they were dodging her. It was not that easy to catch her, and when I finally did and took her to my vet, we discovered that she had pneumonia, heartworm, and badly infected eyes. *And* she was pregnant. She was about six or seven; now she's twelve or thirteen. She has become quite deaf and has slowly gone blind, but she knows every inch of the property and gets around pretty well. She sleeps a lot and eats a lot; she's gotten a little fat. It's the cookies, I know, but cookies are an important part of life.

Some time after Mole arrived, I was driving along a backcountry road when I came upon a small traffic jam with cars stopping and going, stopping and going. When I arrived at the obstruction I saw a tiny piglet of a dog in the middle of the road, confused and lost. An hour later, when I finally caught her, a woman came out of a nearby house. "I thought you would never catch her," she said. "She belongs to the people back there in the trailer." At that, a man appeared from behind the trailer. "You've got my dog," he said. When I explained that I had found her in the middle of the road, he just shrugged. "She always finds her way home." He explained that she had been a neighbor's dog, but that she kept appearing on his doorstep.

When he and his wife returned her to the owner she threw the poor little thing down the cellar stairs, so the next time the dog showed up at their door they kept her. They seemed very kind, but I couldn't bear to think of her on that road. After much begging on my part, they agreed to let me take her.

I named her Ciao-Ciao. She was rail-thin, her front leg had been broken long ago, perhaps on those cellar stairs, and most of her teeth needed to be removed. The little dog had a terrible infection; she was practically rotten inside. Surgery was the only way to save her, but she was so fragile and the operation would be so major that my vet really did not think it was a good idea. At that point I couldn't bear to give her up, so we went ahead. Of course she pulled all her stitches out the day after surgery, but eventually she healed perfectly. Now she's in great shape with one remaining tooth. She's one of the five who like to sleep on my bed, and if the others try to come too close, she curls her lip, showing that one tooth to indicate, *She's mine!* The bigger dogs invariably back off.

Some of my other companions include Milo, a beautiful German shepherd whom I found on a busy six-lane highway. He had been left on the side of the road with a bag of dog food. He was pretty hand-shy and nervous. I have a feeling that the person who left him on the road had rescued him from a bad home.

Then there's Basil, a shaggy dog who spent almost two months on the street in Poughkeepsie until he finally allowed himself to be caught. When I got him, he was still pretty wary, and he snapped like a land crab. He's sweet now. Burr, a huge black dog, came to me from Taos, New Mexico, where my daughter, Erica, found him wandering in the desert with a broken chain

around his neck. Cecil is epileptic; his owners gave him up because they thought he was rabid. Hoover, a lovely gray-and-white feminine Benjy-dog, belonged to a friend of my mother's who hated the dog and was planning to take her back to Animal Rescue—how can you ever take a dog back? Anyway, five minutes after I heard about that plan Hoover was in my car, and I must say she didn't hesitate for a second.

Friday, the Jack Russell, was a real challenge. I have always had a firm rule: I will take any dog who needs a home, but no Jack Russells. It's a matter of principle. They are wonderfully tenacious dogs, but they have been overbred and badly bred in this country, and often they get into the wrong hands. Anyway, this one, Friday, had gone through four homes creating havoc and some bloodshed. Only human blood, but still . . .

Anyway, one day I got a frantic call from a friend whose husband had tried to dispute Friday's theory that anything that fell on the kitchen floor was automatically his. Friday bit the husband, who retaliated by beating him quite severely, breaking a tooth and two toes. There was blood all over the kitchen, and now the man was threatening to shoot the dog. I considered my firm rule and then I went over and picked him up. He definitely did have issues and more than a few bad habits. We had some serious lessons in the beginning, and now he'll do anything for me. I can actually take a piece of meat out of his mouth. When Friday first came to us, I had twelve dogs; he was Friday the Thirteenth. Several months later when one of the other dogs died I told him that now he had a chance to be Good Friday. And so he was.

Recently I found the latest addition, Maggie, a small Brittany spaniel, desperately lost, tired, and hungry. She's beautiful, somewhat fragile, and grateful for her new life. She's a present from heaven, as they all have been.

SASHA

—— Alex Ewing, Retired Chancellor, North Carolina School of the Performing Arts ——

Having read *Found Dogs,* I was already indoctrinated when we first noticed three stray dogs traveling together in our neighborhood. One of them had a collar, and his owner was found; the second suddenly disappeared from sight; the third zeroed in on our block and hung around, day after day. Sheila and I started worrying about her survival, so we put some food in a dish by our driveway, and you can guess the rest.

At first the dog was too nervous to come anywhere near, but she must have been hungry, so after a cautious reconnoiter she would approach warily, eat as fast as she could, and then retreat. After some time I found that I could simply withdraw a good distance, and eventually she would come right up to me—*What's for dinner?*

With my 150-pound Saint Bernard, Samson, and Sheila's two cats, we didn't need another pet, so we got a vet to give the dog her shots and advertised in the paper for a potential owner.

Several days went by before the ad appeared. By then Sasha was ensconced in the yard with Samson, and, cheerful and affectionate, she constantly tried to show us how grateful she was to be with us. When people finally started to call "about that dog you're offering," they didn't seem quite right for one reason or another, and we always found some excuse. "Not sure she's housebroken," or "definitely doesn't like cats," or "we don't know how she is with children . . . " The fact was that we couldn't imagine handing the leash over to a stranger and watching Sasha being pulled into a car, resisting and gazing back with a last wistful or reproachful look.

So I think she's ours now, or we are hers. Which one adopts the other?

HARRY

—— *Nova Lee, Nail technician* ——

One morning I woke up with a premonition. I didn't have a dog at the time, but somehow I knew that "my dog" was at the dog pound; I had to go right away and get him. I canceled my appointments for the morning and drove out to the animal shelter. I looked through the dog pens, then went into the office. I had a clear picture of this dog in my mind, but when I tried to describe him the attendant said, "There's no dog like that here." Frustrated, I decided to adopt a cat instead. As I was driving away with the cat I saw some outside pens that I hadn't noticed before. And there sat a little dog with his paws on the fence. All the others were barking but he was just staring intently at me as if to say, *Turn around and you'll see me.* Of course I did see him, and I called out, "Harry, there you are!" I went right in and adopted him.

He was only six months old and for the first few days he seemed pretty scared, but he was easy to train and well behaved. Soon he was totally adjusted.

I named him Harry for my deceased father. While he was alive, I never got to tell my father how much I loved him, so I thought that if I got this dog and named him Harry, every time I said, "Harry, I love you," somehow, somewhere my father would hear it.

Harry loves to swim, especially underwater. He stays under so long that people think he's going to drown. He likes to pull at roots on the bottom; he looks just like a huge muskrat. Harry also loves to dance. That dog can waltz like nobody else. Right now Harry's favorite is "Connected," by the Stereo MCs. When that music goes on, Harry jumps up and looks at me as if to say, *Hey, they're playing our song.* Then I stick out my hands, he puts his paws on them, and we start dancing. Sometimes we have little arguments about who's going to lead. Harry has learned many tricks. He knows how to play dead, but he absolutely hates that one. He thinks it is so beneath him.

His girlfriend, Heidi, lives next door. She's also from the shelter. They have a great time together, especially since my neighbor cut a hole in the fence between our yards so the dogs can play while we're at work.

I call Harry my sobriety dog. I have been in a recovery program for a year and a half. My life has changed so much, but I could not have done it without this dog. It's Harry—and God—who have helped me stay sober. When you stop drinking you lose many of your friends, so for a while my social life consisted of walks with my dog. He made me get out of the house, and I knew I had to stay sober to take care of him. I made a commitment, and I'm going to keep that commitment.

After all, Harry is the best friend I have ever had in my whole entire life.

SNOWY, TRAMP, AND JAKE

—— Elizabeth Hess, Writer ——

Our most recent acquisition is Jake, the big golden retriever, six years old and 105 pounds. He belonged to a young couple who had a baby and couldn't manage both, so he was on his way to the shelter when I took him home. I knew that he would be easy to place. And he was. He placed himself immediately—in our daughter's room. Kate loved Jake the minute she saw him, and since I am constantly trying to find homes for animals, it was hard to say no when she wanted to keep him.

Actually Snowy is Kate's dog, too. Kate had been begging forever and ever for a dog of her own, so Peter and I decided to give her one for her eighth birthday. In arranging that adoption I did everything wrong; it was a perfect textbook case. In the first place the dog was to be a gift for someone else, and worse still, a surprise. One of the basics tenets of sensible adoption is that a person should choose her own pet. That way there are fewer mismatches and fewer sad confused animals being returned. The next thing I did, definitely not recommended, was to fall in love with a picture in the paper, the Pet of the Week, knowing absolutely nothing about the dog's temperament or history. The shelter staff insisted, quite correctly, that Peter and Kate come in to meet Snowy. The dog was originally a stray who had been adopted by some people who kept her a couple of months until she ate their mattress. They brought her back to the shelter with a note that read, "This dog is neurotic and demanding. We wish her luck."

I wish I could say that from that day forward Snowy was a perfect dog in every way, easy and well behaved, but in fact she was neurotic and demanding. She also was, and eight years later still is, terrified of boots, hugs, and anyone or anything touching her neck.

Tramp was an adolescent puppy who one day followed our neighbors, Charlie and Brenda, when they went out jogging. They found his owners who, as it turned out, really didn't want the dog. Someone had given him to their young son but the boy quickly lost interest in him. "You want him? Take him," they said. So Brenda and Charlie took him home to their house, where he kept them awake all night. Their own dog hated him.

At that point I was doing volunteer work at the shelter every day, so I told them I would take the dog over there. He's very good natured. He jumped right into the car, put his head in Kate's lap, and went to sleep. We were feeling more and more guilty, but we had Snowy and Mr. Tibbs, an enormous white cat formerly homeless, and my husband was miserable with allergies. It didn't seem like a good time to bring home another animal. When we arrived at the shelter, I took him in. The poor dog started shaking. I could see what that experience must be like from the dog's point of view. I just couldn't leave him there.

We could not bring the dog home unannounced because I had sworn never to surprise Peter again with a canine visitor. So Kate got on the phone to explain, between sobs, that we were immobilized; we simply couldn't leave the shelter without Tramp. Somehow Tramp had come to embody the whole dilemma of unwanted animals. I simply could not dump him at the shelter and then go home to make dinner. Peter knew he was cornered but Tramp's precarious future worried him, too, so he said right away, "Bring him home." (Now he says, "Why didn't you tell me he was going to

shed all over everything?") And Tramp is the sweetest dog in the world.

These three dogs are members of our family. They wandered into our lives. All were home-less and perhaps this made the bonds between us tighter. Anyway it's a mutual affair: We are all most content when we are home together chewing bones.

FRANCES

—— *Jamie Lee Curtis, Actor* ——

My favorite pound dog/found dog, Clark, died many years ago. Since then we have adopted big dogs, but for a long time I had been wanting another small dog to be a companion for me. I'm in the car a lot. I have time to spend with a dog. Clark was a cockapoo, so I called some poodle rescue places. I actually went and met different dogs at three different times, but it just wasn't right. They were elderly, and we already have two old dogs. I was amazed that I had the mindfulness to know that it wasn't right, and to do that three times—it wasn't easy, but they were dogs who needed a quiet home, and we have children and big dogs. Sometimes it's kind of a crazy life here.

Then I went off to Texas, doing promotion. Heading for a TV interview, I was in a stretch limo with eight people, people from the ad agency, people from the company I was working for, and a makeup person. We had two hours to kill. It had been on my mind, so I said, "I'm in the market for a small dog. Let's see if there's an animal shelter anywhere around here."

The driver took us to a beautiful building, a shelter that was obviously well run and well funded. Everyone scattered, oohing and ahhing all over the place. I saw an adorable, tiny, pure-bred white cocker spaniel puppy and a bunch of other small dogs, but there was nobody there for me. We all climbed back into the limo. We still had a little time before the interview, about forty-five minutes, so I asked the driver if there was any other place nearby. He remembered a tiny shelter that was right on our way, so I said, "Let's just try there."

We arrived at the North Texas Humane Society, a small building probably not very well funded, though the people who worked there were obviously loving and dedicated to animals and their welfare. I went into the small-dog area, a cinder-block room with metal cages—nothing fancy, but it was clean and well kept. I was walking along looking left and right when one of my companions said, "Hey, Jamie, what about this one?"

I turned to my right and there peeking out was a little black face with cartoon-character-eyebrows. Our eyes immediately connected; I saw her and she saw me. I took her out of the cage and picked her up. She was young, about fourteen pounds, not little, but by this time I was hooked.

I tried to ask all the right questions—How old is this dog? How big will she get? And so on—but I knew the answers hardly mattered. I didn't have much time and even if I had, it wouldn't have made any difference. I said, "Okay, I'll take her."

Someone had given her up to the Humane Society with the sadly common problem, "Moving to a building that doesn't allow animals." Now, maybe that was true and maybe they just couldn't handle having a dog. Who knows?

I decided to name her Frances because there was a statue of Saint Francis outside the shelter. She got the spelling of the crazy movie star and the spirit of the patron saint of animals. I left her at the shelter so that the staff could do the paperwork and give her a bath, and we went on to the TV station for my interview. When we arrived I told my Frances story to the producer who immediately said, "I wish you had brought her along!"

So the people from the shelter raced the dog down there and I carried her onto the show. Afterward we went back to the shelter to finish the paperwork. Then we all posed for pictures in

front of the limo, pictures that were eventually featured in the shelter newsletter. That night Frances and I stayed in the presidential suite at a big hotel in Dallas. The next day we flew home from Texas to California. Frances came home; she has been home ever since. She has melded perfectly into our family, although she definitely knows that I was the one who rescued her.

Now, the truth is that Frances has gotten a little bigger than I had anticipated—she's not exactly a one-hander, she's a one-and-a-half-hander, if not a two. I think she's a little Scottie, a little long-haired dachshund, and a little something else. Above all, she is sweet and delicious.

J.J.

—— Pattie Pankone, Barber ——

One day a drunk showed up at my shop with a three-month-old rednose pit bull puppy on a rope. She was wagging so hard she was pretty near bent in half. I had heard that the guy was abusing her and in fact he had hit her so hard on the top of her head that her teeth had gone right into the roof of her mouth. I didn't argue much about the hundred-dollar price tag. Everyone in the neighborhood knows that I have a soft spot for dogs, so I guess there may have been more than just luck involved when J.J. ended up on my doorstep.

Despite the rough start she had, J.J. loves people, especially kids. In "attack" mode she likes to face-lick them from the chin to the top of the head and whip them hard with her ferocious wagging tail. A friend of mine, a volunteer with the San Francisco SPCA, takes J.J. into schools to help with a humane education program. Everyone says J.J. is really good at her job.

She's not pushy with people but she definitely is pushy with other dogs. She's very dominant and actually dog-aggressive. I'm going to take her back to school to work some more on socializing. She needs it. Any dog is a big responsibility but especially one who doesn't get along with other dogs. She's only three, so I think she can do better.

When I got her all my family had died so I guess she is my family now. She's a sweet dog. I really wanted a German shepherd. Now, isn't that a funny-looking shepherd?

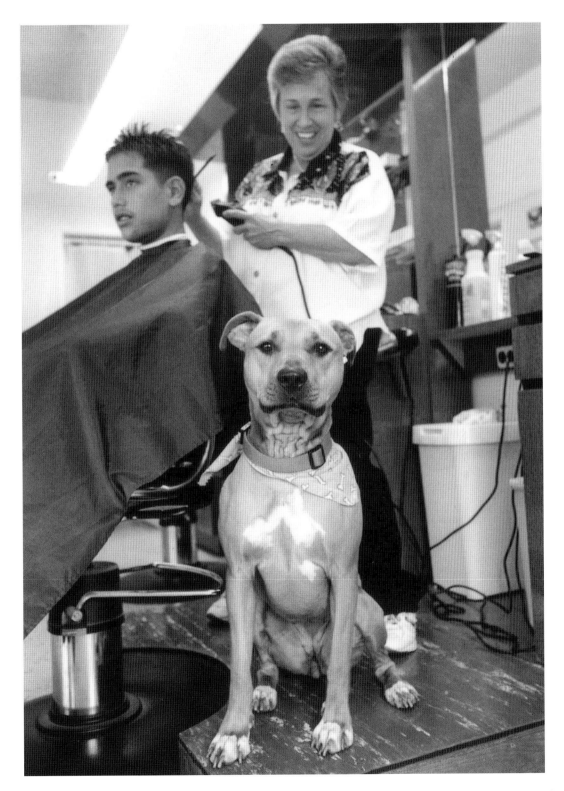

CASSIE

—— *Henry Blagden, Rancher* ——

Awhile back a letter from my East Coast alma mater arrived at our ranch in eastern Oregon. It included a card soliciting information for the alumni news. Since my classmates and I had recently passed the half-century mark, the school was apparently conducting a census on how close each of us had come to achieving life's goals.

I had a vision of a flood of little white cards proclaiming triumphantly the conquering of such lofty summits as senior partner of a prestigious law firm, CEO of a giant corporation, perhaps ambassador to Egypt. My own trajectory looked a bit different.

Being a romantic, and one of life's great underachievers, I concluded after taking personal inventory that a loving wife, three great daughters, a twenty-gauge Purdey shotgun, and a good bird dog made practically anything else in life insignificant. It was the acquisition of Cassie the Pound Dog that made my achievements complete.

When Cassie and I first met, her talents were not immediately obvious. This is not a tale of love at first sight. Cassie wasn't coy; she just took a while to reveal her charms. Our courtship began with a blind date.

Over the years my wife, Sue, has helped the local animal shelter find homes for many stray cats and dogs, so it was not unusual that they called her one morning. I overheard snatches of the conversation: "Gun dog . . . English setter . . . one black ear . . ." and I admit the words did pique my interest. By middle age, however, I was determined that never again would I succumb to the siren song, "Owning My Own Bird Dog." Over the years I had provided homes for quite a variety of these creatures, and as far as hunting, pointing, and retrieving went, all were complete disasters. Among the most notable was the black Lab

who would hunt and kill only cats (which he did exceedingly well) and the Chesapeake Bay retriever who was terrified of gunfire. I had made a pact with myself: No more money down the drain, no more disappointment, no more agonized confessions to a neighbor that his beloved cat had been torn limb from limb.

I still don't know what came over me that morning, but I found myself in the pickup headed for the animal shelter. Cassie turned out to be small and thin as a cartoon jackal. Her feelings had obviously been hurt to such an extent that she could not bring herself to look at me. I certainly knew better, but I brought her home anyway. The shelter manager assured me that I could always bring her back "if things didn't work out."

The next week I went off to Texas for some turkey hunting. On the drive down I considered Cassie suspiciously and wondered how she might embarrass me in front of my Texan friends. The first day, while my host and I were driving around the brush country checking out roosting areas, a pair of bobwhite quail glided in front of us and dropped into a patch of prickly pear. Cassie had not seen them, so just for the heck of it we let her out downwind and—wham! Cassie froze into a beautiful and stylish point. "Well now," the usually laconic Texan drawled, "at least your pound dog's got a nose." And indeed she did.

When we got home I called Tim Ault, a trainer near Boise who has quite a reputation for working with English setters. I wanted him to try her for a couple of days and see what he thought of her. It was obvious that Cassie had had some training, but I didn't know how much or what buttons to push. Besides, all my accumulated failures with her predecessors had left me more than a little gun-shy about trying

my own hand at training. Cassie had already earned a permanent place in the cab of my pickup but it was music to my ears when Tim called to say, "You have a really fine little dog here—she's got it all!"

Cassie stayed at Tim's for two months while I drove the seven-hour round trip once a week to admire her progress and to be trained myself with the dog. Cassie did seem to have it all and a little extra to boot. One of her tricks that Tim had never seen before was to smartly execute a victory roll at a dead run upon the completion of some aspect of her training with which she was particularly pleased.

At last, her schooling behind her, Cassie came home to stay. I wanted to get her on birds right away while she still had a keen edge. Wild chukars were scarce at that time of year so we went to my friend Warren's high-desert ranch, which was stocked with pen-raised chukars and pheasant. We had a great time and returned as often as we could. One day while we were hunting Warren showed up to see how we were doing. Now, Cassie had made a big impression on Warren on our first visit, so when I mentioned that she had been finding a lot of birds, he looked pleased. Then, still grinning, he told me that a few days earlier some hunters from the city had arrived with two very fancy dogs in a shiny new trailer. After a full day of yelling, screaming, arm waving, whistle blowing, shooting, and dog chasing, they had failed to kill a single bird. Warren had not helped matters when he regaled the frustrated men with tales, exaggerated I'm sure, of a certain pound dog from Prairie City, a dog who had hunted there a few days before with great style and flair.

Back home that night I was feeling smug and generally pleased with life. Cassie did some small thing that I considered singularly wondrous, and I made the great mistake of exclaiming within earshot of my wife, Sue, "Oh, you sweetheart!"

"Sweetheart? *SWEETHEART!* You never call me sweetheart!" Sue retorted in a tone that was not exactly cooing.

I did some fast talking, but I must admit I was somehow thrilled that this small white dog with one black ear had managed to energize the spirit of the green-eyed monster in my happy home. Thank goodness, Sue managed to overcome such low sentiments, and domestic tranquility was restored; all jealousy vanished. Or so I thought until several months later when I was visiting Sue's sister and her husband on a trip east. In the course of catching up on family news Sue's sister said, "Now, Henry, I want to hear all about this pound dog of yours who looks like a frog with pink lips."

Ah, well, a small cross to bear for all the sparkling and happy days Cassie and I have had hunting together. She is not as sharp today as she was when fresh from Tim's training. This is entirely my fault, as I am a poor disciplinarian and tend to think that everything Cassie does is unique and splendid. I have gradually realized that she is a much better hunter than I am, so all my directive arm waving and whistle blowing is neither necessary nor productive. The dog seems to know instinctively that I need to keep her in sight if I am to be able to flush and bang away at the birds she points, and she accommodates me pretty well in this regard except when bashing through dense woodcock cover in Maine. There I put a bell and a check cord on her and occasionally regress to yelling and whistle blowing.

Last fall on my way home from one of these Maine "jungle hunts" I was standing in line at the airport waiting to check my bag and Cassie's traveling crate. She was beside me on a leash, flirting with a small boy behind us. He looked up at me and said, "Hey, mister—what is this dog?"

With my best impression of Charlton Heston as Moses, I announced solemnly, "This . . . is the greatest bird dog who ever lived."

EMMALEE

—— *Nanci Ryder, Publicist* ——

Emmalee's mom was thrown from a car on the freeway and rescued by a friend of mine. A few days later the dog had five puppies. My friend brought three of the pups into my office. She knew I would take one, and I nearly took two. I have two Maltese, Franny and Zooey, who have been together all their lives and are totally bonded. They thought it was crazy to take Emmalee, but they have always had each other. Emmalee is my dog.

First I got her, then I got breast cancer, so I have spent a lot of time at home with her. Recently someone asked me to make a list of the things that make me happy. Emmalee was a part of every item on my list. She's fun—she's a lot of fun. She thinks she's an interior designer. She doesn't like trim on anything, and she thinks it's her mission in life to remove it.

I pick up dogs on the street all the time. I carry dog food in the car so I can catch them. I board them at the vet's while I try to find the owners. I look for signs and ask around in the neighborhood where I found them. If I can't find the owners I usually can find a good home.

Emmalee and I met when she was really young, before she was even weaned. And it all worked out for everybody.

Look at her. How cute is that?

ELY

—— Del Webber, Animal lover ——

For many years my fiancé and I would drive from Los Angeles to vacation in the mountains of Idaho. One year on our way home we stopped at a gas station in Ely, Nevada. As we got out of the car to stretch our legs we noticed a young dog staring intently at us. She had the head of a Saint Bernard, the body of a German shepherd, and the tail of a husky. One eye was blue and the other brown. She was mangy, with a ragged coat and very thin, really just skin and bones. She stared first at Vernon, then at me. We looked at each other and shook our heads. We were definitely not in the market for a dog, and besides the car was filled to the rafters.

The lady at the gas station told us that the dog was a stray who had wandered in one day. They had been feeding her for several weeks. We went on our way, but all the way to Los Angeles we could not stop talking about that dog. Later that week she was still haunting us so we set out to drive back to Ely, arriving late that night. The next morning bright and early the young dog jumped into our car. She was very well behaved on the long drive back to Los Angeles. She seemed so happy to have found a home and we were happy, too. We named her Ely.

From that very first day Ely has always been an easy dog, although come to think of it she did chew a corner off the hot tub—but that was the only bad thing she ever did. She got along well with my two cats and the bird. Now she goes everywhere with me. She is such a sweetheart; she is always attracting admirers. People often stop me and say, "What is it?" So we have invented a breed; we call her an Italian elkhound. Sometimes people respond, "Yes, I think I've heard of that breed, but I've never actually seen one before."

Thinking back to the day when we first saw her at the gas station, I remember the way she stared at us with amazing intensity. She made such an impact on us that we drove eleven hundred miles to get her. Actually, you don't adopt dogs, they adopt you.

MONTROSE

—— Suzanne Aton, Designer ——

The Gray Ghost of Montrose Park—that's what everybody called him the first couple of months he was up there in the park. He had belonged to a diplomatic family who simply moved away one day and left him out on the street. Neighbors said that he hung around the house for weeks and then moved across the street into the park. People left food out for him so he did survive, but he became more and more shy and reclusive.

My husband, Justin, first saw the dog one evening when he had taken our dog, Gabby, up to the park. A large gray dog appeared out of the mist and then vanished. Justin wasn't entirely sure what he had seen. The ghost dog appeared again the next night, so we started leaving food for him every evening. At first we saw him only late at night, but as he became more comfortable he started showing up around 5 or 6 P.M., the dog-walking hour. He seemed to be friendly with other dogs, but he wouldn't let a human get anywhere near him.

Justin and I, with Gabby, continued our daily visits. Eventually the dog began to take food from our hands. Then one day he followed us down our street. He would go as far as the cemetery, then sit and watch us walk away. Sometimes when we went out later we saw him lying by the curb where we had left him. Every morning we went back to the park with our hearts in our throats, praying that he had not been hit by a car. A few times we tried just scooping him up, but he always took off.

It was a tough time for us and for the whole neighborhood. The park service wanted him out of there. People from the Humane Society tried to catch him and a group of us even hired a professional trapper, but the dog was too wary and too smart to let himself be caught.

One day in November Justin was at the park talking with a bunch of people including Robin, a friend of ours. The gray dog came up to join the other dogs and happened to get pretty close to Robin. She jumped on him and Justin immediately jumped on top to help her hold him. Someone ran for a dog crate. You would think that a feral dog, or any dog, would bite under those circumstances, and he certainly could have, but he didn't.

The public shelter is so overcrowded that they have to euthanize dogs who are considered unadoptable. Montrose probably would not have lasted there because he was terrified of people so we took him to the Washington Animal Rescue League, a private shelter. Everyone in the neighborhood had been involved in trying to save this dog, and now everyone donated to the shelter to help him. I went over there virtually every night. At first I sat outside his cage and talked to him; then gradually I moved into the cage. I petted him and petted him to try to get him used to me.

Just before Christmas we took Montrose home. The first thing the poor dog did was race for the Christmas tree to try to hide behind it. He managed to knock it over and then he was really frightened. We set up a crate for him with a towel over it so he had a dark little cave. He stayed there most of the time for the first two months. He wouldn't come out if we were around. He might stick his head out, but if you made eye contact he went right back into his den. He was always happy to go for a walk, however, and seemed thrilled to be back in the park with the other dogs. At first we took him out with a collar and a harness. We were so scared we might lose him again. It was almost a year before we

could let him off the leash and be sure that he would come back to us.

He's still a little shy with strangers but he's the sweetest dog ever. From the beginning he never did anything wrong. He even turned out to be house-trained. Now, ten years later, he is kind of spoiled. If he wants to get on the sofa and you happen to be sitting there, he comes up and grunts at you until you move over to make room for him. We're just thrilled that he's happy now and happy with us.

From what we have been able to piece together about his past, we think that he was on his own for over a year. I think he must be blessed.

ROSCOE

—— Debbie and Murray Levy, Bikers ——

When we were first married, we lived with our cats in an apartment. Roscoe served as security system for a junkyard attached to an auto repair shop. We became friendly with the shop owner and got to know Roscoe. We used to bring him snacks all the time. One day we heard that the shop was closing down, and a few days later there was Roscoe, running in the street. We caught him and brought him back to the shop. The owner said, "Oh, we just let him go. He'll be okay." When we pointed out that it was not okay, the guy said, "Well, Roscoe's up for adoption."

So we took him home. We had to carry him up the stairs. He had never been inside a building before and he was terrified. Eventually we tried to introduce him to the four rescued cats. What a fiasco! One of the cats scratched him, and he hated them on sight. So there we were with this dog and the cats in a small apartment. It was a nightmare.

We decided then that we needed to buy a house. While we were looking, Roscoe went to boarding school. We finally closed on a house where he has his own apartment complete with a chair, a love seat, and a color TV so we can all sit together in the evenings. The kitchen is also part of his territory.

The cats get the rest of the house, but we had to put locks on both sides of the door because Roscoe can open it. Actually the cats can, too.

Last spring Roscoe won a prize for Dog That Looks Most Like Owner at the Great American Mutt Show in Manhattan. We all wore black leather.

The first Thanksgiving in the new house our folks came over for dinner, and everyone agreed that we had to thank Roscoe because without him we wouldn't be here in this house. He just wagged his tail politely. Roscoe feels right at home now and, for a junkyard dog, he's become quite a lapdog.

ALEXIS

—— Cydney Cross, Executive director, Out of the Pits Pit Bull Rescue ——

I can't keep my hands off animals and that's been true all my life. When I was a kid we didn't have any pets but I always wanted them. I used to feed the wild cats in the woods behind our house.

As soon as I was old enough I adopted a greyhound. For five years I worked with greyhound rescue; I managed to place 160 retired racing greyhounds. Eventually I adopted Rose, a greyhound/pit bull mix. She's extra special, combining the best of both breeds. Gradually I moved into pit bulls, partly because I love the breed and partly because people just weren't stepping up to help there.

Alexis, one of my pit bulls, was found in a drug raid in Albany. She was totally emaciated, just skin and bones, about a year old, and they had already started fighting her. She loved people but because of her start she was quite dog-aggressive. I really wanted to keep her so I talked to an animal behaviorist who said, "Work with her, do obedience, do agility. These are working dogs. They need a job, something to do with their brains."

So we did obedience, we did agility, and Alexis seemed to be good at everything. She gained confidence and got used to being around other dogs. She's not interested in playing with them but she minds her own business. Eventually she became the first pit bull to be registered by Therapy Dogs International. We visit nursing homes, programs for kids, drug rehab facilities, and jails. Alexis usually gets a big response in the prisons because those guys all know the breed. One man told me the other day that women shouldn't be handling these dogs, but after he watched Alexis shake hands with everyone he said, "You've got the touch, girl."

Alexis especially loves kids; she always seems to go to the ones who are the most needy. Just last week she licked six hundred faces in one day. It must be a record, even for Alexis. She is definitely an ambassador for her breed. And her breed surely needs ambassadors.

In many animal shelters simply being identified as a pit bull is a death sentence, even for puppies. A large percentage of dogs in shelters today are pit bulls. Drug dealers use them for protection and dogfight organizers train them to fight other dogs, often to the death. Dogs who are not considered good fighters are used as bait. Dogfighting in the United States is illegal, but because of the big money involved in betting it is hard to control.

In 1996 a group of us founded Out of the Pits, a rescue haven and adoption program for pit bull terriers. I turned my home into a sanctuary where dogs usually spend at least a month while they are vaccinated, spayed or neutered, and started on obedience training. The dogs stay with me until the right new home is found. We have two rules: We take no dogs who have shown aggression toward people, and each dog we rescue stays at least a month so that he can be carefully evaluated and started on a training program. Before dogs go to a new home I ask myself, *Would you want this dog to be your neighbor?* My dream is that one day every dog adopted from here will have earned a Canine Good Citizen certificate and started some work like therapy or tracking. Pit bulls have very high energy and love to work. Some of the happiest dogs I have placed are with people who do triathlons and let their dogs train with them. Don't try this at home unless your veterinarian thinks your dog is suited for such intensive exercise!

Dogs come to us from all over, but we can only keep twenty at a time. Every day I get

between fifteen and twenty phone calls and fifty or sixty e-mails asking me to take dogs. When I go to shelters every dog seems to be looking at me with hopeful eyes. All I can give most of them is a pat and a couple of biscuits; we only have room for a few.

We have saved many, many dogs. I just wish we could help more. And I wish more pit bulls could end up like my Alexis. She's a happy girl and a pretty amazing one.

As the great animal behaviorist Vicki Hearne said, "It is true that pit bulls grab and hold on. But what they most often grab and refuse to let go of is your heart, not your arm."

Out of the Pits is a nonprofit rescue haven and adoption program for pit bull terriers, P.O. Box 136, Old Chatham, NY 12136. The Web site is www.outofthepits.org.

LOUIE

—— Sally Mann, Photographer ——

Everyone loves Pie best, but I love Louie. He came to me, like all the other greyhounds, from a wonderful woman in North Carolina, Julie Dearmin. Julie runs Circle of Friends Greyhound Rescue, and a few years ago she found Pie for me, the first greyhound after the death of my beloved Eva. Then she sent me, in rapid succession, Shadow, Bella, Honey, Katie, Baby Dodo, and, last of all, Louie.

Louie had been in a shelter in West Virginia. He had lived in a crate for a year while prospective adopters came and went but no one ever chose him. Finally his allowed time was up; if a dog is not adopted within a certain period he has to be put down. The women who worked at the shelter were distraught. None of them could take on another dog but they could see beneath the scruffy exterior that Louie was a special dog.

So they called Julie, home of last resort for greyhounds in need. Julie lives in a large, rambling old house. When her mother willed the house to her I can hardly imagine that she envisioned it filling with dogs, but so it has. Julie has greyhounds whom nobody else wants: sick greyhounds, old greyhounds, damaged greyhounds, and, like Louie, just plain unwanted greyhounds. Julie cares for them all tirelessly, allowing her own needs to go perilously unmet in the process.

Julie described Louie to me as "just one loving old soft hound"—and so he has been. From the day he arrived, crate-ratty and overwhelmed, he has never been less than a perfect gentleman. He allows Pie, the perennial puppy, to chew his sensitive ears and bite his legs while he smiles with chagrin, a gentle giant of a dog. We shake our heads in amazement and gratitude when we think of how many people walked on by his crate and how lucky we are to have him.

OBE

—— Bob Langendoen, Trainer for search-and-rescue dogs ——

Four years ago my wife, Sue, and I got a call from a local Labrador breeder. She had some potential clients interested in buying one of her pups for their fourteen-year-old son, who had just obtained his hunting license. The problem was that the boy already had a dog, a white German shepherd, and the parents felt that he shouldn't have two dogs. Of course the German shepherd couldn't hunt, so he would have to go. The breeder knew that we had shepherds and thought we might know someone who would take the white German shepherd so that she could sell one of her pups. Unusual for me, I bit my tongue and did not ask how she felt about selling one of her dogs to a family who treated their pets as disposable objects. Instead I told her that we did sometimes hear of people who were interested in shepherds and that I would like to take a look at the dog. Arrangements were made for me to go the next day.

When I arrived at the house, Otis greeted me. His coat was matted and covered with mud, and his pink nose was so badly sunburned that he was a prime candidate for skin cancer, but he seemed friendly enough. He came right up for a pat on the head. He was four years old but beyond that information I really didn't learn much about him from the owners. Questions about what games he enjoyed or what toys he liked brought only puzzled looks and blank stares. These questions were important to me because games and toys are vital tools in training dogs for search-and-rescue work—and for almost any kind of training.

The owners agreed to let me take the dog for the weekend to evaluate him for search and rescue. I had already decided that, no matter what happened with the evaluation, I would never return him. On the way home I stopped at the vet's office to get a copy of his records. They showed various puppy shots and a notation that he had been hit by a car at the age of four months; no further treatment.

At home we observed him with our other dogs and were pleased to see that although he was an intact male he was not aggressive or dominant with our other males. He was a little nervous indoors and terrified of the slippery vinyl floor in our kitchen, not too surprising since he had never been in a house before. He was much more people-oriented than I had expected.

On the search-and-rescue evaluation he performed well on our first exercise, but then became more interested in hunting ground squirrels. I noticed, however, that he frequently put his nose up, sniffing the breeze to see what might be ahead. This behavior was encouraging because it showed that he knew how to use that nose. Now I just had to show him that the object of the game was to find people, sometimes to save lives.

Sunday night I called his owners to tell them that Otis had found a new home. He had also found a new name, Obe, short for Obadiah Goodfellow. I had known an Obe many years ago, a dog who was gentle, loving, and sweet, a dog who'd deserved a better owner. Goodfellow is the name I have given to all my dogs, and it has always fit them well.

That first week Obe went to the vet to be neutered; while he was under anesthesia, the vet took X rays of his hips. When she looked at the films she was puzzled. A second vet came in to take a look. They ordered another set of X rays, which were exactly the same. Then we realized that we were seeing the full extent of damage that had been done when the puppy Obe was hit by a car. His femur had been punched

through the pelvis; it was held in place only by muscle. He has two broken vertebrae, one at the base of his neck, the other at the end of his spine. Both vets agreed that the damage was beyond repair. Having seen the X rays, we were all amazed that he could walk—and trot, and even run!

For four years now Obe has been part of our family, and he is certainly one of the best dogs I will ever own. He has learned obedience, he visits nursing homes and shut-ins as a Delta Society–certified therapy dog, and he has passed all the tests and evaluations to become a fully operational member of our search-and-rescue team. Of course, he has some baggage from his youth—don't we all? He sometimes panics on a slick floor, he still likes to chase ground squirrels, and his structure will never be normal. However, he is my happy-go-lucky best friend and an ambassador of goodwill as a demo dog at our obedience classes, and on searches looking for people who are lost and need our help.

CINDY LOU

—— *Marcie Blagden, Student* ——

One snowy December morning when Mom was getting ready to take me to my afternoon kindergarten class, my sister Eliza called to say that once again she had forgotten her lunch box. I was thrilled to be going to the junior high because I liked to play on the "big-kid swings" while Mom ran in with Eliza's lunch. This time Mom asked me to stay in the car since we would be leaving very soon, but I got out and began making snow angels. A little black puppy face appeared above my face, and a little pink puppy tongue started licking me. We played for a while until Mom returned. I introduced her to the puppy; then Mom and I climbed back into the car. As we pulled away that puppy barreled out in front of us, forcing Mom to stop, get out, and carry her over to the far end of the playground. But the puppy was too quick for us once again and we had to stop.

Mom and I then decided to walk down the street and ask about the little dog at some of the neighboring houses. At first no one seemed to have any idea where she had come from; then we talked to a man who said she had been hanging around for a week or more. He thought she either had been dumped or was extremely lost. Mom and I headed to the police station. They put a notice out over the police radio and told us to take the dog home until someone called.

Days turned into weeks and weeks became months. Sometimes I had nightmares that a person would call to say that my Cindy Lou was actually theirs, their long-lost puppy. I secretly plotted a series of lies in case I should need one someday. But luckily I never did.

For thirteen years Cindy Lou has been with me through everything. If no one else wanted to climb trees, she would fight her way up to be with me; if no one wanted to hear any more of my incoherent poems, Cindy would curl up close and listen attentively. When I went away to boarding school I was afraid she might forget me. By then she was completely blind, and I was afraid that maybe she wouldn't recognize me.

Then, home again after months and months of being gone, I walked into our kitchen and called her name. I heard a loud yelp and sure enough, skidding around the corner came my Cindy Lou, bumping into everything in her path, squealing and yelping hello. Now that I'm in college I hope that these excited hellos will always welcome me home, home with my Cindy Loulou.

PERCY

—— Abigail Lufkin, Graduate student in social work ——

Last September my best beloved four-year-old German shepherd, Jonah, died very suddenly. Anyone who has ever loved a dog knows what this feels like. I was completely devastated. Many people said to me, "You must get another dog right away." And I seriously considered doing just that. The problem was that I didn't want another dog. I wanted Jonah back.

A few months went by. Then my friend Sue adopted a dog from Robin Faber, a woman who has a store near here and does a lot of rescue work on the side—actually considerably more than just on the side. When Sue told Robin about Jonah, Robin promised that, when the time was right, she would find a great dog for me. From Robin's point of view (she is always frantically looking for good homes) the right time was right away.

So periodically Robin would call and leave me messages about various dogs. I would call back and tell her that there really was no way I could adopt a dog at that time as I spent all day either at work or at school. I didn't have enough time, it wouldn't be fair to the dog, maybe in the summer . . .

Then one day Robin left a message about a rottweiler-shepherdish dog who had been rescued in south-central Los Angeles. "I have the dog at the shop with me today. Why don't you just stop by and see him?" *No harm in just seeing him*, I thought. My boyfriend says this was tantamount to sending an alcoholic into a bar.

Well, Percy was about six months old and had been living for several months on the streets in a tough neighborhood. He was little and skinny but so affectionate—all he wanted to do was sit in my lap. So I said, "Okay, I'll foster him for the weekend but I really can't keep him." I spent the weekend playing with him; by the second night he was sleeping on the bed. Still, I said to my friends, "You know, I can't keep him." "Uh-huh, sure," they said. I guess everyone knew Percy wasn't going anywhere except maybe from the bed to the couch.

I found out later that when Percy was only about four months old, a teacher had noticed him hanging out across the street from her school. She started taking him food, and she called him Wiggles because his whole body wiggled with happiness when he saw her coming. Even though he was obviously starving he seemed to be mostly interested in being petted, in interacting with his new friend. At first he wasn't scared at all, but gradually he became more timid and cautious. Sometimes he disappeared for days. Finally the teacher happened to meet Robin and, worried about what would become of Wiggles/Percy, the two set out to catch him. He was nowhere to be found, though they did pick up three other dogs who were not so shy. Finally they met some kids who knew where the dog usually hid, and they helped catch him. Apparently he was terrified, rolling his eyes and trembling. He had a large bump on his head and had most likely had more than one bad experience with people.

This wonderful kind teacher then took him home, where for three days the dog did almost nothing but sleep and eat. Then he perked up and began to play with her dog and enjoy life a

little. Robin saw him and called me. Then Percy and I had our blind date and started living happily ever after.

People always say to me, "It's so wonderful that you rescued him. How lucky he is!" The truth is that we rescued each other. I had no idea how sad and lonely I had been. Percy was like a magical antidepressant for me. I loved coming home to him at night, taking walks in the early mornings, and snuggling together on my big, once-white, bed.

Everywhere Percy goes, from the dog park to Beverly Hills, people love him. "What a kind, gentle dog, what a beautiful boy!" Just last week, a woman said to me, "How lucky you are!" She was exactly right.

MEMPHIS

—— *Anna Deavere Smith, Actress, writer, professor* ——

I don't really know why I got interested in having a dog, but some time ago I started asking people on the street about their dogs. The next thing I knew some friends had found Memphis for me at the North Shore Animal League. She was not exactly a surprise because the people from North Shore had to interview me first to make sure that I was okay.

When I first saw her, Memphis was a tiny puppy, about six weeks old and not quite eight pounds. She is white and black with many different colors of brown. Her ears are brown and soft, and she has fantastic eyeliner. I call her the Diva Dog. She was an adorable puppy, with a funny sideways way of looking at me, almost as if she was slightly suspicious.

When Memphis was still very young, we left New York to work in Los Angeles. When we settled in there, Memphis played a big part in making me feel at home. I have lots of friends in and around LA, but getting together is more complicated than it is in New York. In New York you can call a friend at the last minute, hop in a cab, and you're there. In LA it's more of a trek. Memphis was always waiting for me at home. She was good company, and I felt that we were off on an adventure together.

Being an urban person, I'm used to walking from one point to another to accomplish something, but in LA people usually don't walk anywhere. In fact, at first it felt weird to be walking down the street with Memphis. People would stop their cars to ask what kind of dog she was, or to say they've never seen a dog with so many different colors. Can you imagine people in New York stopping their cab to ask about your dog?

Memphis is a little over a year old now, and she is just beginning to be slightly more mellow. She loves people and she loves other dogs, with a few exceptions. When we meet high-strung, snobby, yappy little poodles, she walks right on by as if they simply don't exist. In our building there is a tiny, tiny poodle with jewelry and bows who screeches at Memphis, but she totally ignores him. In that building, if you can't hold your dog in your arms, it must ride in the service elevator. Memphis loves the service elevator. All the men who work in the building are her friends and they spoil her. How am I ever going to train her not to jump on people when these guys are always encouraging her to jump up to greet them? Memphis is part Australian cattle dog—she's a working dog, and she doesn't mind at all that she can't take the front elevator with those little poodles.

I'd like to write a book, *Memphis Goes to Hollywood*. She could talk about Hollywood and say things that I couldn't. People would receive it better from the mouth of a dog, because they love dogs and they trust them. In a way Memphis has become an extension of my intelligence. Her presence makes me see people differently, like the people who stop their cars to say, "Gee, I never saw a dog with so many different colors." It's significant that I'm an African American person, and so the dog becomes an extension of all of that. She's an interesting figure in my life, even more than a friend, partly because she doesn't speak. Of course, I often assume that she thinks the same way I do. Still, she does give me a different perspective.

POPSICLE

—— *Rudy Carr, U.S. Customs canine enforcement officer* ——

Popsicle had a pretty rough start. When he was still only a puppy, a cop discovered him in an abandoned freezer during a midwinter drug raid in upstate New York. The young pit bull was covered with blood, emaciated, nearly frozen, and nearly dead. That drug dealer had apparently used him as "bait" while training fighting dogs. Organized dogfights with heavy betting are out there all over the country. Sad to say, the drug dealer eventually got off with probation for animal cruelty.

Popsicle was taken to a shelter for some serious medical attention. The staff there loved his sweet personality but the sign on his cage said PIT BULL, and potential adopters were stopped in their tracks. People just walked away. No one wanted him.

So when Popsicle finally recovered and was strong and healthy, the shelter contacted U.S. Customs Canine Enforcement Officer Sally Barr to see if he might qualify for the U.S. Customs Dog Training School. The Customs Service recruits one thousand dogs each year, 90 percent of them from animal shelters. Those chosen represent only a small percentage of the dogs actually tested. Most do not make the grade, but Popsicle played an outstanding tug-of-war, just what Barr was looking for, so he was one of the lucky ones. He went off to school, where he became a star. He was trained to alert to marijuana, hash, cocaine, and methamphetamines. After graduation he was sent to a port of entry on the Mexican border in Texas. Popsicle had

been there only two months when he discovered 3,075 pounds of cocaine on a pineapple truck crossing the border. It was the largest drug bust ever at that port of entry. Popsicle was a hero. He even got a medal. It's just so great that he's getting back at the bad guys like that drug dealer who starved him and abused him.

Popsicle is quite a dog, a real ball of fire, and he loves to work. It's all a game to him. We play training games four or five times a day to keep the dogs interested. If they don't make finds pretty regularly, they get bored and discouraged. We use a towel saturated with synthetic narcotics scent. When the dog finds it, he gets to play tug-of-war and he always wins. He also gets a lot of praise, physical and verbal. The handler has to be enthusiastic; we say that whatever you're feeling runs right down the leash. Popsicle is not a pet, he's my partner.

Drug dogs usually work for eight to ten years if they stay healthy. Then, at retirement, the handler gets to take them home. I sure hope Popsicle is still with me when he retires. I'd like to take him home, pamper him, and make sure that he's happy in his last days. He deserves it.

To commend the U.S. Customs Service for the praiseworthy policy of seeking out shelter dogs to train for enforcement work, contact Lee T. Titus, Director, Canine Enforcement Training Center, U.S. Customs Service, 828 Harmony Hollow Road, Front Royal, VA 22630-9302. The e-mail address is Lee.T.Titus@customs.treas.gov.

TIMMER

—— Lara Babalis, Flower designer, musician, and paramedic ——

When I got Timmer, he had been at the pound for seven months. Everyone there loved him. They said they always knew that he would be adopted. He just needed to find the right person. He was about two years old and had been found wandering as a stray. He was featured in the local paper as Pet of the Week, and when I saw that face I went right down to the animal shelter and took him out for a walk. After the walk, he stood there and leaned against me. I said, "Obviously you're mine."

He probably came from a farm or ranch. He is definitely a herding dog; he's always trying to herd the horses at the barn where I ride. When he first moved in with us, he tried to herd my six cats, but cats really don't herd very well. We are all currently living with my mom. Fortunately, she loves animals. She points out that, while her sister's house is in *Architectural Digest*, hers will be in *America's Funniest Home Videos*.

When I went away for a week, Timmer stayed with my boyfriend at the firehouse. While he was there, he learned to "stop, drop, and roll." Now he goes with the firemen to do fire safety demos at all the schools. The kids love him.

He goes to work with me every day. He's always busy and almost never alone. He's so intelligent and so active that I'm sure he would get into trouble if he was bored and lonely.

He's a lucky dog, and he absolutely knows it. Besides, everyone's always telling him so.

LUCA

—— Felicia Funke-Riehle, Writer ——

My mother collected children and dogs, so perhaps it was inevitable. For a long time, however, I had not followed in her footsteps. But one day, not long before Christmas, I noticed a dog lying in the street, flat on its belly, dirty and ragged looking. I thought it had probably been hit by a car. People at the dry cleaner's said she had been there all morning but no one seemed to take much interest in the poor thing. I couldn't just leave her there, so I decided to take her to the vet. A kind man lifted the dog and put her into my car. For thanks, she peed all over him, terrified.

When we arrived at the animal hospital they took her in for observation. She crawled a little but seemed unable to use her hind legs. We thought perhaps her spine had been injured. The next day, when I returned to see about her, the vet told me that she had apparently been beaten severely. He had never seen a dog so traumatized, physically and psychologically. She did not move, eat, or drink. She lay in the cage, facing the wall, her back arched in a strange way. She was about nine months old.

I called the animal shelter to see if they would take her. They said that they had many dogs there far more adoptable than she, and that they would probably have to euthanize her. Wolf, my husband, said, "Let's take her home and give her some time, give her a chance."

I thought it was a great idea, but the vet said that in his opinion it would be very foolish, especially since we have a young child. "You have no way of knowing how this dog will react. It could actually be dangerous to have her in your home. Probably the best thing for her, and for you, would be to put her to sleep."

Despite this very sensible advice, we decided to take her home with us. We didn't know how it would turn out, but we thought that if the dog improved enough to eat and have a quiet life, it would be enough.

At home we put Luca's basket in the entry room at the front door, which is a quiet place as we generally use the back door. At first she just lay there, limp, facing the wall, shutting herself out of the world. She would not look at us or even move if anyone was there. We concentrated on making her comfortable and tried to be quiet around her. Fynn, six years old, sometimes forgot and bounced about, but he was the first person to whom she responded. He broke the spell.

Our Rhodesian ridgeback, Ito, looked after Luca from the very beginning when she seemed not to know what to do with other dogs. We think she had been completely isolated, no contact with other dogs and very little with humans. Ito loves all dogs. I could have brought any dog home and he would have been kind to it. Once Luca got used to him, I think he made her feel more secure. If Ito wasn't scared of things, perhaps they weren't so dangerous.

Luca didn't do much for the first two months. Then one day she crawled on her belly from the entry into the kitchen. We couldn't believe it. What a milestone!

We started taking her on short walks in the neighborhood, but if someone shouted or a door banged she would lose all confidence and run for home. We could not put a leash on her. She became completely panic-stricken at even the sight of one. We had to be careful about our body language—no talking with our hands. She was nervous in the car, constantly pacing, exhausted by the time we got home. Even so, I took that poor dog everywhere—to school, to the post office, to the store. I was determined to help her get socialized.

Now, almost a year later, it is amazing to see the change in her. She's happy. She adores Wolf, and he spoils her. When they sit together watching TV she gently puts a paw on his arm or his shoulder. Sometimes he holds her paw. She sighs with happiness and gazes at him, looking like one of those baby seals with soft eyes. He used to think that dogs should stay in their place. Luca has certainly changed his idea of what that place should be.

She is such a good dog. She can sit and lie down when we ask her. She always comes when she's called and never wanders. She's a good companion for Fynn. They go on many expeditions together. She's an incredible dog. She has added so much to our family. And to think that I could have assumed that the wretched little dog lying in the street was really none of my business . . .

JESSE

—— Mikhail Baryshnikov, Dancer • Lisa Rhinehart, Dancer, homemaker ——

Jesse is a Florida girl. Our friend Rose, who lives on a farm down there, found Jesse with her litter of pups living under an abandoned car. The dog was about a year old, scared and nervous, but Rose went back every day with hot dog bribes (this was not the first dog she had rescued), and eventually she managed to get mother and puppies into her truck and back to the stable.

The puppies were adorable, as puppies always are. People loved them and soon all were adopted, but nobody wanted Mum. Jesse had a name now but she was a bag of bones, fearful and shy. She had never had a home.

About that time we came to visit. We went riding every day with Rose and her pack of eight dogs, including Jesse, who trailed behind the others, definitely at the bottom of the totem pole. She was afraid of everyone, humans and dogs, but at the same time she wanted to be included. Watching her struggle with this conflict was heart wrenching. After a week of seeing us every day, Jesse began to warm up, and although she was still timid, she seemed happy to see us. We were touched and flattered.

Our old dog, Tim, had just died at the age of eighteen. He was a stray we found wandering on the streets of Manhattan. We knew that we didn't want a puppy because the kids were so young, but we did want another dog at some point, though perhaps not so soon after Tim's death. But there was Jesse; she needed a home, we wanted to help her, and when our visit ended we took her home with us.

It was a difficult transition for her. For several weeks she stayed in one corner, hid out really, and would go inside and out only through the door where she had first arrived. Gradually she became more comfortable although even now, eight years later, if someone new comes to the house she disappears. She loves the snow, but she's terrified of thunderstorms. We call her Nostradogus because she will actually predict a bad storm. Two days beforehand, she goes and hides somewhere, trembling for hours. She probably saw some terrible storms in Florida when she was living in the wild.

She is a sweet dog, both needy and grateful. We fell in love with her—how could you resist?

SWEETIE

—— *Mark Welsh, Writer* ——

One dark night about four years ago a small black-and-tan dog turned up on the doorstep of my farmhouse. She was in pretty rough shape, pitifully thin, covered with ticks and fleas, and very neurotic, too, as many abandoned dogs are. I somehow managed to catch her, not an easy feat, and next day took her to the vet to ask his advice on what to do with her. "Ah, put her to sleep. It's the kindest thing." Instead I put signs up around the town, FOUND, SMALL BLACK-AND-TAN DOG . . . I prayed that someone would claim her. Then I tried to give her away. No such luck.

For the first month she wouldn't come into the house or anywhere near me. She lived up in the woods and came down only to eat. I don't know how long she had been on the road. I picture her like a swagman with a little kerchief tied on a stick over her shoulder. I imagine that she had been on her own for a good long time, considering her condition and her wariness about people. She wasn't a bit shy about chasing the neighbor's cattle in the paddock over the road.

Eventually she became calmer, and she acquired a name, Sweetie. I must say that at first she had very little natural charm. Then, like one of those slow-motion photo sequences where a flower unravels from a bud, she really did blossom, revealing layers of personality. Perhaps they had been there before; perhaps she now felt comfortable enough to have those layers revealed.

After several months of settling in, we moved into New York City. Sweetie was freaked out. She hated the noises, the buses, the collar and leash. I took her to Washington Square Park, three blocks from the apartment, hoping that other dogs would distract her. I even took off the hated leash so that she could gambol about.

Some loud noise frightened her and she took off, dodging through heavy traffic to run the three blocks back to the apartment. It was one of those dreadful cinematic moments where I actually watched the cars narrowly missing the dog. By some miracle Sweetie arrived at our building unharmed. At that point I was finally convinced that she was meant to be in my life, and since she did head for the apartment when she panicked, I suppose she had decided that I was meant to be in hers.

After her near escape I realized that I had to teach her some basics, such as *come, sit,* and *stay,* and somehow she had to realize that I was the boss. Within one afternoon she was doing it all, and since then she hasn't looked back.

At that point her story, and mine too, took a slightly unpredictable turn. I had just left a job in the advertising business, so Sweetie and I went to Europe to see the fashion collections. My friend Jon Bartlett was showing in Milan along with many other top designers. Sweetie loved being in a civilized country where dogs were welcomed in restaurants, and she enjoyed the shows as well, especially backstage where the models and photographers hung out. When Sweetie jumped on a model's lap, suddenly all the photographers were around that girl. The next minute all the girls were calling, "Sweetie, oh Sweetie . . ." She was very much in demand as a lapdog, and within a week or two her photographs were turning up in magazines around the world—Tokyo, Moscow, Paris, and New York. Her name was getting out there as a fashion dog, and whenever anyone asked I told them her rags-to-riches story. Here was a dog who had been abandoned on the side of the road—and now she was traveling to Italy, sitting on my lap at fashion shows, and staying at

hotels where all the fabulous people were staying. Sweetie took to this glittering life, especially the part that involved eating steak in restaurants. She always sat quietly and never touched the food on anyone else's plate.

Back in New York many people knew her. She always sat with me in the front row at Jon's shows, sometimes on Julianne Moore's lap, sometimes on Sarah Jessica Parker's. When those pictures were published I saw the potential of a girl from nowhere writing an accurate and satirical commentary on the fashion business. I submitted a column proposal to *Elle* magazine, and within a week Sweetie's career as a columnist was launched. She became *Elle*'s four-legged fashionista, providing a bit of silli-

ness in an industry that takes itself so seriously.

She had a cameo opposite Joan Rivers in *The Intern* and a walk-on for *Sex in the City*, which didn't make the final cut. For one of her columns she was photographed wearing a two million dollar diamond necklace from Harry Winston. Harry Winston has become Sweetie's official jeweler. Her book, *Sweetie: From the Gutter to the Runway* has a chapter on accessories with advice from Sweetie to "match your rocks to your roast beef." It features a picture of Sweetie in an elaborate ruby necklace (Harry Winston, of course) sitting down to a very rare steak. All the photographers say that she is great to work with. When she is in front of the camera, she doesn't move from the position and just gives you different angles. She's a pro. Sometimes friends accuse me of being like a stage mother pushing her, but when she's working you can see that she enjoys it. Of course she gets a lot of extravagant praise, and she loves it just as the human models do.

I guess I gave her a new life (however reluctantly, at least in the beginning), and she has done the same for me. Writing the column, the book, and now a second book, and looking into merchandising, licensing, cinematic and televi-sion properties, and more, I have a new career, a career centered on Sweetie. Best of all, I work every day with my best friend.

Sweetie's books:

Sweetie: From the Gutter to the Runway, Tantalizing Tips from a Furry Fashionista, as told to Mark Welsh, Warner Books, 2001.

Sweetie says . . . I Never Met a Man I Didn't Lick, as told to Mark Welsh, Stewart, Tabori and Chang, 2002.

MINNIE MOUSE

—— Lisa McElhinny, Retired fishing guide •
Wilson McElhinny, Retired international banker ——

One day in mid-October we went out to a nearby hiking trail where we found a delegation from the local animal shelter with a bunch of dogs, all hoping that someone would take them for a walk. We spotted Minnie tied to a tree. A nice German shorthaired pointer, she looked as if she needed a walk so we took her with us. We hiked up the canyon for several hours and had a picnic. Returning down the trail in the afternoon we removed Minnie's leash and, of course, she took off after the next mountain biker. We raced after them, thinking we might have lost this beautiful dog, but mercifully she stopped when she reached the shelter group with the other dogs. Greatly relieved,

we went home. The next day each of us, unbeknownst to the other, turned up at the shelter to visit Minnie. By that time we were entrapped. Our vet took a look at her, pronounced her healthy, and she was ours (and we were hers).

Minnie has made us a family. She loves to run and has turned out to be an ideal cross-country skiing companion. She runs ten miles every day while we try our best to keep up with her. At home she is the most mellow, lovely dog, with only one fault: She tends to be so affectionate that it's hard to ignore her. Obviously we're crazy about her, and she seems pretty happy. You could call it a win–win situation.

DAKOTA

—— *Mike Lingenfelter, Construction manager* ——

Several years ago I had two serious heart attacks and several major surgeries. I was diagnosed with unstable angina, which is painful and scary. I went into a deep depression, I lost the will to live, I bottomed out. Drugs didn't help; nothing helped. Finally my doctor and my psychologist recommended a therapy dog. In years past we had various family dogs, but never one who was actually mine. I was not particularly enthusiastic about the idea of getting a dog, but then I was not particularly enthusiastic about anything at that point. Anyway, we heard about a golden retriever who had gone through basic training as a therapy and assistance animal. My wife, Nancy, and I went to see the dog. He came out with a green rubber frog in his mouth, and he was obnoxious. He constantly wanted me to do something with him, and he was always hauling things around—you know how retrievers are. I couldn't stand him, but Nancy said, "Let's just try it for the weekend." I reluctantly agreed, but I had made up my mind that he would go back first thing Monday morning.

Naturally, by Monday morning Dakota had won me over. I had even begun to see how his "obnoxious" behavior was just what I needed. His job was to make me do things, to force me to get involved with life again.

Dakota had come to the Golden Retriever Rescue Club of Greater Houston when he was found tied to a post in some lady's yard. He had a very bad case of heartworm, and in fact had almost died when his heart stopped during the treatment for it. When he recovered, Texas Hearing and Service Dogs took him for training, but their physical exam showed that he had an old injury, a broken hip, probably from an accident with a car, making him ineligible for their work. So it was back to Golden Retriever

Rescue, where they arranged to have him trained for therapy and assistance. Then we got together, thanks to my doctors. They really had the right prescription that time.

Dakota got me back to the world again; he saved my life. In the first place I had to take him for walks, which meant that I had to get out of my chair and actually leave the house, something unusual for me at that time. Then, since Dakota was certified by the Delta Society as an Animal Assisted Therapy dog, I started taking him to work in special education classes serving children with Down's syndrome and other serious learning disabilities. He helped those kids learn colors, and how to write their names.

One day in the middle of a school presentation Dakota started to act up and fuss. I was pretty annoyed with him. I was taking him out of the room when I had an attack. I didn't see the connection until the same thing happened a few days later. I finally realized that Dakota was letting me know when I was about to have a heart attack. Apparently, when an attack is gearing up, the heart puts out enzymes that cause an odor. The dog had figured out that this was a bad thing and displayed his anxiety. Another time he woke us up. My blood pressure was seriously down, so low that Nancy called 911. Dakota had given me some valuable time. He had become my guardian angel.

He lets me know anywhere from two to five minutes before an attack, which gives me time to take some drugs. Then, if he settles down, I know the drugs are working. These alerts have let me have a normal life again. I've been able to go back to work, since Dakota goes, too. One day he actually alerted on one of my coworkers, a man who had never had heart trouble. The guy at first thought Dakota was crazy, but then he went into the first stages of a heart attack. Now each day at work everyone wants to say hi to Dakota and get a sniff test.

A few years ago Dakota got the Delta Society award for Service Dog of the Year. He and I have worked with Delta to educate people about the importance of access for service dogs. Everyone recognizes guide dogs with blind people, but I have an invisible disability, which means I may get an argument when I try to take Dakota into a restaurant, a library, a school, or even on public transportation. Dakota and I have been on TV many times, including on the Discovery Channel and Odyssey. We work hard to teach people about service dogs.

Dakota's life has changed a lot since that day when he was abandoned, and mine certainly has changed, too. I never knew that angels came with big brown eyes and long bushy tails.

For more about Dakota, see *The Angel by My Side,* by Mike Lingenfelter and David Frei; also the Web site www.angelbymyside.com.

The Delta Society is a human service organization. Its mission is to promote the role of animals in helping people improve their health, independence, and quality of life. The Web site is www.deltasociety.org.

PHOTO: Gay Glazbrook

TOMMY TRUE AND FRANCES

—— Rae DeVito, Realtor ——

My first deaf dog was Pollyanna, a dalmatian. Communicating with a deaf dog was a bit difficult at first. I learned to use hand signals, eye contact, and lots of physical reassurance and reinforcement. Soon after Pollyanna died, I heard about Frances, a six-month-old deaf dalmatian puppy in Los Angeles. A man had found her abandoned on the street. He couldn't keep her himself, but was paying to board her at an animal hospital and visiting her there every day. I called him. He told me all about the dog and sent photos. I wasn't really ready for another dog; it was too soon after losing Pollyanna. But I just couldn't say no.

As it turned out Frances needed companionship and a lot of it, so I was already thinking about a second dog when the vet told me about Tom, the albino Australian shepherd. Tom had been born on a ranch, mostly deaf and partly blind. The rancher had thought it best to kill the puppy at once but his kids said, "No way!"

They named him Tom. Tom got along pretty well until he was attacked by some dogs and badly hurt. The vet fixed him up and in the process became attached to the pup. By this time I had a bit of a reputation, for better or for worse, as someone willing to take care of deaf dogs. I went to see Tom and decided to take him even though I had no experience with blindness.

Tom has limited vision. He sometimes bumps into things but in general he gets around fine. He seems to see Frances' black-and-white better against green grass than he does in snow. He notices a shadow across his face. His sense of smell is highly developed, probably because he relies on it so much. At first I kept him on a leash whenever he was outside. Gradually he began to follow Frances.

The two dogs have become friends. They sleep together and bring each other little gifts. Frances is quite protective of Tom. If he seems confused about where I am, I point to him and Frances goes over immediately. Then he usually follows her; they come back side by side.

I try to touch Tom frequently. I use a lot of physical reassurance, petting, and treats, because, "Good dog!" even in the most enthusiastic tone of voice means nothing to a deaf dog. Frances notices my facial expressions and responds to them, or at least she does when it suits her.

Tom has our regular creek walk memorized. He knows where all his watering places are. He shoots down the path, runs circles around the meadow and then takes a hard left to the creek. He often bumps into me or Frances or passersby but he certainly knows his grid. When he first came he was very cautious about terrain changes, but now he slides down banks and even runs across small ditches. I ski cross-country all winter. Tom follows my tracks in the snow. Once in a while he detours after someone else, but when he realizes that it's not me, he returns to the place where he left me or, as he probably thinks, the place where I left him. "Why can't that woman pay attention and stay on the track?"

People sometimes ask why I keep getting these handicapped animals but I don't think of them as handicapped. They're just my dogs, Frances and Tom. They are interesting companions. Frances is definitely a character, and Tom is an inspiration. He finds happiness so easily.

When I watch him grab a tiny stick and leap into the air or race past Frances, tears come to my eyes. It's a picture of absolute joy.

I do spend a lot of time with them, but it's very rewarding. Everything here is theirs, including me.

JET A. DAWG

—— Rebecca Haggie, Airport operations agent ——

Jet came to Southwest Florida International Airport from Border Collie Rescue Incorporated, an organization that finds homes for border collies who have been abandoned by their owners. Unfortunately there are a lot of border collies out there in need of a home. They look so great in the movies that most people forget that these are working dogs. The Border Collie Rescue Web site describes them as "fanatical black-and-white dogs that have been bred to herd sheep." Most of them need serious work and a great deal of exercise. One owner says, "As long as I throw the squeaky ball for her five or six thousand times each evening, she seems pretty content."

Dr. Nicholas Carter, the founder of Border Collie Rescue, started training the dogs for goose control on golf courses and corporate parks and then realized that they could help prevent bird strikes at airports, Right now about half a dozen commercial airports plus various military bases in the United States, Canada, and overseas use these dogs to protect birds, airplanes, and the traveling public.

Jet was a pioneer, the first dog to be used in wildlife management at a commercial airport. He was very good at his job; after all, herding is what he was born and bred to do. He just lives for birds, and they probably see him as some kind of stealth predator because he doesn't bark, and he can run up to thirty miles an hour. Birds don't become desensitized to a dog the way they do with noisemakers or pyrotechnics. The dog works with a handler like me. We use standard sheepherding voice signals to direct the dogs. We try to place ourselves in a position where the dog can move the birds in the direction we want them to go. Jet has all the standard intensity of his breed, so it's not hard to keep him focused. He's also an excellent PR dog—friendly and photogenic, great with visitors and the media.

The program here was a real success, but after only two and a half years on the job Jet was diagnosed with a degenerative heart valve condition so we had to retire him. You would never think he had a heart condition because he acts more like a seven-month-old puppy than a seven-year-old dog. With a special diet and medications he will probably have a normal life span, but his work just required too much running.

When Jet retired last year he came to live with me, and it's been quite a challenge to figure out how to keep him busy. Footballs and basketballs make pretty good herding objects; he can't pick them up so he noses them around and works them that way. Sometimes he even gets me to kick them for him. Big excitement! He's become a self-appointed watchdog; he owns me and the house. He's jealous of my two whippets, who *were* here first, but never mind. They just kind of put up with him as he tries to wiggle in between us. At my house, if you pet one dog, you pet three.

I've been around animals most of my life, particularly dogs and horses. In high school I was a veterinary assistant. I have to admit that Jet is pretty unusual; learning about the border collie mind has been fascinating. Besides all his intensity the dog is a ham. He makes me laugh every day.

To learn more about Border Collie Rescue, go to www.bcrescue.org — "Do I Really Want a Border Collie?"

POINTER

—— Rick Slone, Writer ——

We were visiting friends in San Diego, me and my son Cary, then fifteen. This was four years ago, and I happened to overhear a comment he made to a friend of his: "My mean old man," Cary was saying, "will never let me have a dog."

His mean old man!

We'd talked about a dog several times over the years. My answer had always been that with Cary at school and me at work, what would the dog do all day? Stay cooped up in the house alone? What kind of life was that? I also understood, Cary's protestations to the contrary, exactly whose dog it would be. I'd made the same empty promises to my own parents. Kids love the idea of a dog but their idea seldom includes feeding it or walking it, much less picking up poop. I also knew an untrained dog could be a nightmare. A humper of legs, a howler, a chewer of shoes and furniture legs, a roamer. Cary had only a vague recollection, but when he was small and we lived out in the country, we had a beagle, Pie, who was all those things and more. Cary didn't remember that Pie impregnated our neighbor's purebred white German shepherd, and so in addition to the incorrigible Pie we had five of his offspring. No, there'd be no dog for us.

But to be called "the mean old man" didn't sit well with me either, so I agreed to look at a dog Cary's mom had found. I would go through the motions, appease the kid, but no way were we getting a dog.

We drove to Oceanside, forty-five minutes up the freeway. To this day I don't know why we were selected, Cary and I. Great good fortune is my best explanation. There's a waiting list years long for dogs like Pointer. He was two at the time, a golden who'd been through eighteen months of training in the Canine Companion program, but had washed out because, of all things, he was too playful. He couldn't stay focused on his work, not with another dog around to play with.

His trainers, Mike and Sue Calvert, put him through his paces for us: all the usual stuff—sit, stay, come, heel, and then some extraordinary tricks—he could turn on the lights! Open the fridge! Pee on command! You'd point, he'd pee! He came with an instruction book. Thirty commands. But the clincher was *cuddle*. Told to cuddle, he'd plop down on your lap.

How could you not take a dog like that?

As predicted he's become my dog. He's with me twenty-four hours a day. At the office, at the coffee shop, at the skating rink. He sleeps on my bed. At my ball games he sits in the dugout, comes out to take my glove from me when I come in from the field.

In December 2001, during what we believed was routine surgery, Dr. Karsten Fostvedt found a tumor in Pointer's colon the size of my fist. It was malignant, he was sure. It was very bad. Did I want to put Pointer down then and there, spare me and him the agony? Both Cary and I felt we had to give Pointer a chance, regardless of the odds. The biopsy confirmed the vet's prognosis: The tumor was malignant, it was virulent, almost certainly it had already spread. Pointer would be dead in a matter of weeks.

During Pointer's recovery from surgery, Cary and I sat in his kennel with him. Karsten gave us the keys to the clinic so we could be with him at night and over the weekends.

Pointer had a stream of visitors who brought him stuffed animals he loved. A round of chemotherapy followed.

That was thirteen months ago. Pointer's alive and well. No sign of the cancer. Karsten saved his life. At the clinic they call him "the miracle dog." Karsten says that a dog like Pointer makes being a vet worthwhile.

My girlfriend claimed I loved Pointer more than I loved her. Love Pointer more than I love you? I said. Not true. As much as, maybe, but not more. I thought this was the highest compliment, an expression of my deep feelings for her. She didn't see it that way, understandably, I suppose. Not everyone is a dog person. Before Pointer I wasn't either. She's gone now, but Pointer, he's still here, asleep at my feet as I tell his story.

MAMMA, HONEY, ET AL.

—— *Natalie Owings, Sanctuary director* ——

A few years ago, after twenty years of rescue work, I established The Heart and Soul Animal Sanctuary, a no-kill, nonprofit refuge for abandoned animals—dogs, cats, turkeys, llamas, horses, donkeys, and chickens. I believed then, as I do now, that the power of love is the best way to reclaim animals who have been damaged by abuse. That means treating the dogs, by nature group animals, as cherished family members in a group home environment. I don't believe in locking them up in pens or cages. This only promotes anxiety, loneliness, and howling.

So I live in the Giant Dog House, one big room with thirty dog beds and one human bed, my own. If a new dog arrives full of fear, she is comforted, fed, reassured. When night comes, she sometimes sleeps beside me, desperate for loving human contact; sometimes she is still too frightened. Days, weeks, or even months later, the dog begins to smile and play; her scars begin to heal. I talk to them a lot. I think it's important. The more comfortable you make animals,

the more at peace they are and therefore the more adoptable.

I find homes for dogs all over the country. I screen these people carefully—after twenty-five years in this business I can tell a good home or, for that matter, a bad one. Dogs stay at the sanctuary anywhere from two weeks to sixteen years. If they are too old or too traumatized to be adopted, they stay here forever.

I have rescued dogs all over New Mexico and Arizona. I have found them abandoned, thrown from cars, in traps, starved. I have scraped them still alive off the highway. Many of the dogs I rescue have been hungry all their lives. Many have received harsh treatment. I try to replace sadness with happiness, fear with love and respect.

As Albert Schweitzer wrote, "A man is ethical only when life as such is sacred to him—the life of plants and animals as well—and when he devotes himself to helping all life that is in need of help."

SAGE

—— Alfred Johnson, Student ——

One day I saw an ad in the paper for a dog at the animal shelter, a dog who seemed like our own dog, Sunny. When Mom and I went down there to have a look, the first pen we saw was full of a variety of puppies. Sage with her seven brothers and their mom had been abandoned in an apartment when the puppies were only three weeks old. Sage was the first one I picked up. She seemed like such a good dog, we just took her home with us. By then she was ten weeks old, the only female in her litter, which gave her points with my mom from the beginning. If Mom was at all willing to get a puppy, I certainly wasn't going to argue with her about which one to take.

Right away Sage was amazing; she was just so smart. Only a week after we got her she could already sit, lie down, and shake. Now, at three years, you wouldn't believe the things she understands. She knows right where the house key is, and one day when we were going for a walk, Mom said, "Sage, where is your collar?" Sage raced off and came back with the collar.

She's quite the athlete; she can jump really high. One day she cornered a deer in the backyard, and she often catches chipmunks and squirrels. She traps them with her paws, but when she grabs at them, they always escape.

Even our old dog, Sunny, likes her okay, though Sage is a little bit of a pest. She only bothers Sunny to try to get her to play.

Sage has always been a little shy with strangers but she absolutely loves some of my friends. She is incredibly devoted to the whole family. She just wants to be with us all the time. I think she keeps getting better and better all the time. Sage is just a really cool dog.

KIPPER AND FRIENDS

—— Robin Faber, Store owner ——

A park ranger rescued Kipper from some kids who were trying to drown him in a swimming pool. As you might imagine the dog had major issues. For a long time I couldn't touch him—no one could—and if anyone approached, the scared little thing would retreat to a corner and put his paw up in front of his face.

Lily was in the worst shape of any of my dogs. I found her in East Los Angeles. She was foraging for food while these guys were throwing bottles at her from a balcony. When I rushed in to grab her, they started yelling at me, but we got away before they could get down from the balcony. She had such terrible parvo and worms that she nearly died. I climbed into her cage at the vet's every day to tell her that she had to live.

Hopper was living with some people who were going to have him put to sleep because, at six months old, he had chewed some flowers. He would have been the third puppy these people had killed for one reason or another.

I found Debbie under a car waiting for her drunk owner. I absconded with her and her one remaining puppy. Debbie fell in love with my boyfriend, Mark, but she had serious separation anxiety issues. Every time Mark went out, she destroyed the house and once even managed to escape to try to follow him. Mark found all this irresistible, and he's kept her ever since.

For most of my life I had never thought much about rescuing needy animals; then, seven years ago, I found a stray dog on the street. I couldn't keep him at my place, but I didn't have any idea of how to find a home for him, even though he was a wonderful dog. Shortly afterward I found another one. Then Mark and I moved into a house, a big house, with a big yard. That very first week I took a wrong turn

and ended up down by the Los Angeles River where I ran into a chow mix and a pit bull who were running around looking for food. People in the neighborhood told me that they had been hanging around for a few weeks. The two dogs were happy to jump into my car so I took them home, opened the gate, and then thought, *Oh my, what have I done?*

From that day forward I have never been without a couple of dogs in need of homes, but as I look back now, it was ridiculous. I didn't know what I was doing, I didn't know how to place the dogs, I didn't know how to get help with spaying and neutering—I didn't know anything. Now I have a whole system for rescuing dogs; still, most of the expenses come out of my pocket. When people adopt, I ask for a donation, which usually doesn't even begin to cover the costs of vet care, spaying or neutering, vaccinations, mange treatments, collars, leashes, tags, bedding, food, flea and heartworm preventives . . . Some of the dogs I rescue have serious medical problems and huge vet bills. I have a dog right now who needs a two-thousand-dollar bone surgery.

The two vets I work with are wonderful, very understanding and supportive. They do everything they possibly can to help, and I couldn't do this work without them. The city gives out coupons for spay and neuter—thirty dollars for a dog, twenty dollars for a cat—but a low cost spay averages a hundred dollars for a dog, about eighty for a cat. This year they are issuing only two-thirds the number of coupons.

Sometimes people who adopt will make an extra donation, or sometimes I meet someone who wants to help. To a large extent this whole project is a dependence-on-the-kindness-of-strangers thing.

I have five dogs of my own and six cats, so I can usually bring a couple of dogs to live with me. I work with some low-cost kennels, and I have volunteers who go there to walk the dogs and socialize them. I'm always looking for good foster homes, but the turnover is pretty high. People often fall in love with a dog and decide to keep it; after this happens a few times they don't dare foster anymore. I place dogs primarily through word of mouth and ads in the paper. Over the years I have become quite intuitive about people, even from phone messages. I probably only return about one-third of the phone calls I get. If I like the sound of the person, we arrange for a meeting with the dog. Then if everyone gets along, I do an interview

with a house check, and there's an application and a contract.

Over the years I have become more and more committed to the importance of spay and neuter. Money spent here is a great investment; it saves so much in the long run, both in dollars and in preventing hardship. I frequently go into low-income communities to persuade people to let me take their cats and dogs to be spayed and neutered. I work with a small group of women in various neighborhoods. These are people who try to help abused, abandoned, and stray animals even though they usually have absolutely no resources whatsoever. Often they are struggling themselves. Some of these people are a little crazy, but, you know, seeing so much awful,

awful stuff can make you crazy. The problem is so huge, the need is so overwhelming.

Recently I've had to stop taking pit bulls. They can be wonderful dogs but they are so hard to place. I have to admit, though, that I do have a pit bull right now staying in my girlfriend Shalott's garage. But this dog was at death's door, and we couldn't leave him there to die on the street. He was torn and tattered, encrusted with scabby mange. There was not one hair on his body, he was missing an eye, he had mutilated ears, and one leg was completely twisted. He must have had the most hideous life. When we managed to get the dog into the car, he was completely unresponsive. We talked about euthanasia—in this case it might have been more practical. He looked like some kind of monster. You could barely touch him, and the smell of mange was appalling. For days he showed no dog-like behavior—no recognition, no tail wag. But Shalott has nursed him along, and he's doing pretty well now. He's the one who needs the two-thousand-dollar bone surgery. He's very sweet, like a goofy old man, and I have faith that someone will eventually fall in love with him.

ROCKY AND MINNIE

— *Peter Quinn, Antiques dealer* —

Rocky has been with me for years. He came to me when he needed a home because his owner was going into the military. Rocky is a tough little guy, but he does suffer from separation anxiety, and when he does, we all suffer.

I thought a canine companion might help him so I went to the local humane foundation, where I found Minnie. She had been adopted several times, but always returned. She's a nice little dog but extremely competitive for attention. Rocky and I were her last chance, and for some reason she decided that it was okay to share me with him. Rocky and I have an unbelievable bond, and Minnie and I are getting there.

Minnie had been brought to the shelter originally by a drunk. She still cowers if you raise your voice, even if it has nothing to do with her. The shop has been very good for Minnie, and the dogs have been very good for the shop. It's a great place for socializing them, not that Rocky needs any socializing—he's crazy about other dogs and women. Both of them work hard every day greeting customers and alerting us to the threat of dogs presumptuous enough to actually walk past the store window.

These two have certainly stirred up my life.

CINCO

—— *Annette de la Renta, Dog rescuer • Oscar de la Renta, Fashion designer* ——

Oscar: I was on the road between the airport and our house in the Dominican Republic. Local fishermen often stand near a bend in the road to sell their fish.

Annette: They like that place because there's a big sharp curve in the road, and cars have to slow down.

Oscar: Anyway, I saw this man with a plastic bag in his hand. I thought I might get some fish for our dinner so I stopped to ask what kind of fish it was. The man replied, "It's not a fish, it's a dog."

I was horrified. "What do you mean? How can you have a dog in a plastic bag?" Then the man showed me this tiny, tiny dog.

I negotiated a price, and I asked this man to take the dog out of the bag and to hold it for me while I went home. We already had I don't know how many dogs in the house, but when I told Annette what had happened, she said, "You must go right away and get this puppy!"

We called him Cinco because it was the fifth of December. He was a tiny, tiny baby, very furry even then and quite dark. Since coming north he has become much blonder.

Annette: He's become a WASP dog.

Oscar: This dog Cinco actually has the nicest nature of any dog. You don't know any dog more loving; he's unbelievable. Typically, and like all our other dogs, he adores Annette. He follows her everywhere. Sometimes he goes outside with me, and when he comes back in, even after five minutes, he goes desperately looking for her. He runs around frantically and goes into every room until he finds her.

Annette: He's so scared of being ditched.

Oscar: No, I don't think so, because he could be with me but it's not the same thing. In addition to being so loving, Cinco is extraordinarily intelligent.

Annette: He's intuitive more than intelligent.

Oscar: No, he's very, very bright. Every night he comes to this chair, and he lies down here. Then when I come up—you know, this is my chair—I say, "Cinco, please give me my chair," and he goes and sits there on the sofa. Every single night.

He's only bad in the streets on a leash. He's scared of other dogs and he gets aggressive.

Annette: The unfortunate thing is he's terrified, and the way he manifests it is to get aggressive. But really he doesn't want to fight.

Oscar: Besides Cinco we have two other dogs here and six more in the Dominican Republic that Annette is trying to place. There were fourteen of them. These six all need homes but as you know it's much more difficult to find homes for dogs once they're not puppies anymore. Also we have three dogs of our own at our house on the beach there. There's Saba who looks like the Egyptian god Anubis, all black and elegant, and Sophie who's sweet. Lucky is the emperor of the whole beach. He is part Rhodesian ridgeback, strong and good looking.

Annette: They are all wonderful in different ways. Cinco, I think, is the most grateful. Lucky, on the other hand, thinks that we're lucky. And he's right.

BOBBY BLUE

—— Peter Howe, Photographer ——

Bobby Blue is a seven-year-old Samoyed. Some years ago when he was quite young he was picked up by the cops on the street in Long Island City with no ID of any kind. They took him to a shelter in Queens, and I heard about him through Samoyed Rescue on the Internet. I adopted him and immediately started taking him to obedience classes. It was the trainer there who suggested that Bobby seemed to have the perfect temperament for pet therapy.

So five years ago, after Bobby was evaluated and certified, we began visiting hospital patients with cerebral palsy. Then just six months ago, through the Good Dog Foundation, we started making weekly visits to pediatric patients at the Institute for Neurology and Neuropathy at Beth Israel Hospital. The kids we see there have had brain tumors, brain stem surgery, and spinal surgery.

Bobby has his own photo pass just like the doctors' passes. On a typical day, when we arrive at the hospital the security guard says, "Hi, Bobby Blue!" People in the elevators speak to Bobby by name. (Usually nobody knows my name.) We go directly to the pediatric ward where they give us a list of kids to see—the kids who would most enjoy this big fluffy toy that moves. Most of the patients here are in bed, so it's a little tricky trying to get Bobby close to them. Sometimes I put him on a chair next to the bed so the kids can reach him. I carry a Polaroid camera so that I can leave souvenirs of the visit.

Then we go to the intensive care unit. The staff throughout the pediatric unit has been very supportive and enthusiastic. Not only do they allow us to go into intensive care, but they actually insist that we do. Again, they give us a list of patients to visit. Recently we were there when I noticed a little girl lying on her side facing away from us. When I told the nurse that we would go around to the other side so that the child could see Bobby, she asked us to stay where we were because they were about to turn the girl, and it was going to be difficult and painful. As they moved her, the child started crying. She cried and cried until suddenly she spotted Bobby. Then she started to smile. It was amazing.

We usually go from intensive care to the day treatment floor where kids come in for chemotherapy and other procedures. Here it's easier to get close to the patients. They can pet Bobby and shake hands with him.

People say that they don't know how I can bear to go to the pediatric units, but I find it incredibly inspiring. These kids are going through a terrible time, but they have such spirit. And Bobby helps them. Samoyeds were originally bred in Siberia, where one of their duties was to guard the children. You might say that Bobby Blue is genetically programmed for this work.

For more on The Good Dog Foundation and Animal Assisted Therapy, visit the Web site: www.thegooddogfoundation.org.

CHELSEA, RED, AND CLYDE

—— *Tracey Rice, Restaurant consultant* ——

I grew up in New York City with five dogs, a capuchin monkey, and assorted fish. Chelsea was my first pit bull mix. She was a stray lucky enough to end up at the San Francisco SPCA, where she spent four and a half months before I found her. She's fourteen now, my heart and soul. We have been through a lot together, and Chelsea is my angel. She doesn't like to be bothered now so she's the invisible one in the photograph.

I spotted Red one day when he was hanging out in a park near the projects. He was a young dog, about six months, a bag of bones and very shy. For a couple of weeks I tried to lure him with cookies and Chelsea, but whenever I approached him he took off. One miserable cold rainy day my husband, John, and I were walking with Chelsea. We go out no matter what the weather is. The only other thing alive in that park was Red, skinnier than ever and shivering. We scattered cookies around, and when the dog came over we lassoed him with the leash. He was scared to death, shaking, very unhappy and fearful, but for some reason he didn't bite us. We took him home, dried him off, and fed him. John pointed out sensibly that we really didn't know anything about this dog.

The next day I took Red to seven different animal shelters. It was the same story everywhere: We will take him, but we will have to euthanize him. John and I decided then that we would have to keep the dog and try to rehabilitate him. Red came from a tormented life but he has turned into such a lapdog. He is twelve now, calm and happy though things still scare

him, things like buses and trucks and the vacuum cleaner.

Over the years I have found homes for many dogs, especially pit bulls and pit mixes. Sometimes we foster the dogs until a good home turns up. John loves animals but he's not nearly as obsessive as I am. He thinks that two pit bulls in one family are enough dogs.

Then two years ago Bonnie and Clyde, two tiny pit bull pups, were left one night in a box on a groomer's doorstep. We agreed to take them and try to place them. I put an ad in the paper, but most of the people who called were looking for guard dogs. I didn't have a good feeling about any of the callers until a nice woman who had lost a beloved pit bull fell in love with Bonnie.

Clyde has stayed with us. He's two years old now, a prince of a dog and very handsome, red with a white muzzle, bib, and paws. He is fun and funny and he loves everyone. I take him to visit group homes for foster children. The kids are great with him. They love to make him go through his repertoire: *sit, stay, down.* He works for cookies.

I have concentrated on pit bull rescue because they are the ones who need the most help. There are just so many of them, strays and castaways, dogs kicked out of fighting rings because they were unsuccessful fighters or no longer useful for bait. They seem to find me one way or another. I guess I'm an ambassador for the breed—and my dogs are, too.

DAISY

—— *Courtney MacDonald, Fabric artist* ——

Daisy used to live in a pretty tough area of East Los Angeles. When she was still quite young, her family moved out leaving her in the backyard with no food or water. Of course she barked and cried—*Where was everyone?* After a day of this the woman next door put a pot of water on the stove, and when it was boiling, she carried it outside and threw it on Daisy. At that point one of the other neighbors took pity on the dog and brought her to a vet in the neighborhood. He said he couldn't even look at the animal without a two-hundred-dollar deposit. This was impossible so the woman took the dog home and did what she could to make the poor little thing comfortable. She fed her and put baking soda on the burns. The next day she called Robin, guardian angel of abused and abandoned dogs. When Robin saw Daisy she was horrified, and Robin has seen a lot of horrors. She says the dog was just one big smelly scab. Her boyfriend said, "Robin, you will *NEVER* find a home for this one!"

After some time at the vet's, Daisy spent days recuperating behind the counter at Three Bags Full, Robin's sweater store, which is where I first saw her. When I came into the store with my daughter, Daisy was lying there. Her eyes were running and oozing. She had no hair at all on her face, under her chin, or on part of her back. Her skin was still blistered and red. While my daughter tried on sweaters, I sat down with Daisy behind the counter. As I petted her, she rolled over so that I could scratch her tummy. Then she licked my hand. I saw dogs at that store all the time, but Daisy was something special. I think it was love at first sight for both of us.

So I said to Robin, "I can't take her today because I have a house full of people, but if she's still here next week when they've gone, I will take her."

Well, she was still there—I think Robin must have saved her for me—so I took her home for a few days to see how she would do at our house.

At first she was a little nervous. She was afraid to take food from your hand. Even today she backs up if you offer her food with your hand. She didn't like grass—I don't think she had ever seen it before—and she was scared of Merry, our big pound girl. Victoria (a Chihuahua/Maltese cross who adopted my husband) was pretty grumpy. Nevertheless, by the time the few-days trial period was over, Daisy had all of us under control.

She just got better and better, and her fur . . . Well, we weren't sure if the hair would ever grow back, but now she has the most extraordinary coat, including a white daisy on the top of her head. She loves mud and muddy water and she hates to be fussed with so I keep her clipped pretty short.

She has become quite a huntress. She likes to sleep with her nose in the doorway to keep track of what's going on outside, and when the squirrel is in the bird feeder, she sits back and waits until he jumps down. Then the chase is on! I think both of them consider it a great game.

Recently a friend of Robin's who had seen Daisy when she was first rescued saw her again; the woman burst into tears. She couldn't believe it was the same dog. Now there is even a rumor that she's a Tibetan terrier. Apparently these dogs were never sold; they were given away as good luck. If she is a Tibetan, I don't know how she ended up in East LA.

But she's been good luck for me. She's my girl and I spoil her as much as I can.

WOLFIE

——Stiles Colwill, Interior designer • Jonathan Gargiulo, Antiques dealer ——

We did not find Wolfie; she found us. Her life at Halcyon Farm began early one morning nine years ago. A large black-and-white dog appeared behind the garbage cans, much to the upset of the resident pack of Jack Russell terriers. Tired, thin, and very nervous, she clearly had seen better days.

We gave her water and food and left her alone for a rest. Within a few days she had summoned up enough courage to move indoors to the back pantry. Several days later she progressed to the kitchen. It was several months before she felt brave enough to go upstairs where we all sleep.

Something very bad in her past life may have involved stairs; she couldn't bring herself to put even a paw on a step, until one night when she marched right up with us.

Over the years she has earned the title, Nanny, as she helped nurture and train four litters of Jack Russell puppies. Her more routine duties include announcing and greeting everyone who enters the yard.

Along with brood mares and foals, barn cats, house Russells, and rottweilers, Wolfie enriches our lives and adds to the daily adventure of life at Halcyon Farm.

ROSE AND ANGUS

—— *Laura Apshaga , Chef* ——

I wasn't sure that I was ready for a dog. I didn't even go near the shelter the first three years that I lived here because I was working so hard. My hours were long, and I just didn't have time to give to a dog. It takes a lot of time, especially in the beginning.

Then, when my boyfriend, Jared, was helping out at the shelter one day, he came home and told me about this great dog. The very next day a friend at work said, "Laura, there is a dog at the shelter that you must see." It seemed that two people in two days telling me about the same dog must mean something, so I went down to see her, and brought her right home with me.

Rose had been at the shelter for several months, probably because people are scared of any dog that looks at all like a pit bull, although Rose is so sweet that I can't imagine anyone being afraid of her. I think she might be a British Staffordshire terrier, shorter and stouter than an American Staffordshire. Where the ears came from it's hard to say. When we left the shelter I heard someone say, "Who's adopting the pig?" So rude!

Before the shelter she had been with an abusive family. Two of the kids ended up in the hospital after trying to set each other on fire. The dog was kept chained to an old car, often without food or water. Some of the neighbors used to feed her and bring her water.

At my house she spent most of her time in the closet at first. She seemed to think it was the only place safe enough to go to sleep. She definitely had issues. She hated loud talking and still does, even if you only raise your voice in a discussion. One day Jared called her "Bat Dog" on account of her ears, and she ran off and hid in her closet, shaking. She must have thought that he was saying "Bad dog!" She and I had an odd relationship for the first few months. She loved my roommates, but she always seemed leery of me. We just didn't bond. I couldn't reprimand her, even gently, for anything. She wouldn't come when I called, just hid in the closet or under the deck. It was horrible.

I tried to spend a lot of time with her and did everything I could think of to reassure her. Finally, after almost eight months, it began to pay off. Since then she has really blossomed. Even with what she went through, she likes everyone, especially babies and kids. Jared and I sometimes take her to visit people at the nursing home. They love her because she is so friendly and so gentle. The last time we were there she offered her paw to someone to shake. She had never done that before. The old man was thrilled, and so was I. She is just so cute.

After Rose had been with me about a year, I went out to the shelter to look for a cat because we were having mouse problems. Rose likes cats. While I was there one of the attendants said, "Have you seen the rottweiler puppy?" He was a big fat thing in a cage out back. Eight months old, he had been given up by owners who loved him when their landlord said he was too big and had to go. They should have figured that out before they got him. I came back three different times to look at cats. The third time, I brought Rose along to meet the puppy. She liked him. She licked him on the nose, and we adopted him instead of a cat. I changed his name from Conan to Angus.

The first month was hell. Angus had been neutered just before we got him and was wearing an Elizabethan collar to keep him from trying to take the stitches out. The house was tiny, and he banged into everything. Then his inci-

sion got infected. Rosie had a mange attack brought on by stress. Angus started escaping from the yard, chewed everything in sight, and dug up the lawn. Meanwhile, both dogs ran laps around the house, inside and out. I began to have second thoughts about keeping him. I talked to the shelter manager, and she urged me to give it some more time. I am so glad she did, because he is the sweetest dog.

He particularly loves babies. He will go and sit by a stroller with his head turned upside down on the baby's lap, gazing up into her face. He seems to understand that a baby is not just another animal, or maybe he would be as gentle with any baby animal.

He and Rose are totally devoted to each other. They play, and then they curl up and sleep together on their own couch.

The dogs are definitely a commitment. Sometimes it's hard when my work schedule involves long hours, and I do like to snowboard. I usually take the dogs with me. They don't mind staying in the car, and then they are ready if I have time for a quick walk. Often at the restaurant they stay in the yard. Sometimes they lie outside the kitchen door and watch me work.

RAGS

—— Bets Simon, Golfer, skier, dog walker ——

I call her Rags, short for Rags to Riches. I found her at the local shelter, where she had been abandoned by her previous owners. They said that they simply couldn't be bothered with a dog. I can't imagine how they could have felt that way about any dog and especially about this one. She has never been a bit of trouble here.

When I brought her home, she was very shy. The first day she hid in her kennel and didn't come out at all. Eventually she decided that a little dinner might be a good idea. Then she found the dog door and let herself out. She was perfectly housebroken from the beginning. Gradually she began to feel more at home, but still it was weeks before she wagged her tail.

Now, six months later, she seems confident and secure. Sometimes she has puppy fits and races madly around the house in a burst of energy and exuberance. She likes to be with me. When I play golf she supervises the golf cart, and at home she sits on my lap for hours. She loves to travel and thinks a private jet is just fine, a totally appropriate accessory for such a good dog.

LUCY

—— Bunny Williams, Interior designer ——

The story of Lucy is a true life story of love at first sight. I wasn't looking for a dog; in fact, I didn't even want a dog. I had two dogs, and the last thing I needed was a third.

My friend, John Rosselli, and I were in Atlanta on a trip looking at the great classical architecture of that city. I was not even thinking about dogs as I sat on a bus with about twenty other people from the Institute of Classical Architecture. Well, then someone ran out of film, the bus pulled into a shopping center, and the driver happened to stop right in front of the Three Dog Deli. Somebody said, "Oh, look at all the dogs!"

Of course, I rushed off the bus. There were three pens filled with all kinds of dogs, but I only had eyes for Lucy. She was just having the best time, bouncing all over the cage—so happy, so alert and so excited, a red bandanna around her neck. I bent over and she jumped right up into my arms. She was adorable and I was in love.

But I had to get back on the bus to go on with the tour. Someone had a cell phone so we called the Three Dog Deli to ask about the person responsible for the terrier with the red bandanna. A surprised woman called Bren came on the phone and I explained who I was, that I lived in New York, and that I wanted to adopt Lucy with the red bandanna.

"Well, that's impossible," she said. "We never let our dogs go out of state. Anyway you would have to fill out the application on our Web site before we could even discuss it."

There I was, on a cell phone on the bus, no computer in sight. We continued on the tour, visiting one wonderful house after another, and all I could think about was Lucy. I was obsessed.

That night we had dinner in another beauti-

ful house. Our host was showing me around; we went into the library and there on the desk I spotted a computer. This nice man immediately agreed to look up petorphans.com, where we found a picture of Lucy and the application form, five pages long with many very, very personal questions. I filled out the form on the spot, but knowing that I had to leave the next day, I decided to call everyone I knew in Atlanta to ask them to call Bren to say that I was okay, that I really was a great dog lover, and that it would be fine.

The next morning I woke up at five o'clock, but since it was Sunday I waited until nine to call Bren. The first thing she said was, "I thought it was going to be you. I have had about twenty calls vouching for you so I guess it's okay for you to adopt Lucy."

Bren is a remarkable woman. She always has five or six dogs in her house getting in shape for adoption. She goes to various shelters in Georgia and Alabama looking for likely candidates. Lucy, when she found her, was in terrible shape, with a big wound in her side and almost no fur. In six or eight weeks the wound healed, her coat grew in, and Lucy was ready to look for a permanent home. Then she went off with me, leaving Bren an empty slot so she could go and look for another dog.

When Lucy first arrived at our apartment, Charlie (mutt) and Brewster (elderly Norfolk terrier) took about ten minutes to inspect her while she rolled over submissively and seductively. Even John's whippet, Elizabeth, liked her.

Lucy is a very, very special dog. She loves people; she's always happy, always busy. She's independent but at the same time very loving. Sometimes when I'm trying to read the paper, she jumps right in my lap—and I love it! Once

in a while, if it's raining and this independent terrier doesn't want to go outside for a walk, she hides under the bed. But she has a tail that never stops wagging—thump, thump, thump on the floor. You can always find her.

You know, if I were a sensible person, I might have gone back to New York without Lucy, but I took one look at that dog and knew I was not going to leave Atlanta without her.

I definitely believe in love at first sight.

In 2001 Bunny Williams and Kitty Hawks produced the first annual Great American Mutt Show in New York City, a consciousness-raising event dedicated to increasing public awareness of the importance of adopting both mixed-breed and purebred dogs from shelters as well as supporting animal welfare organizations nationwide that encourage adoption of animals and support spay/neuter programs. See the Web site www.tailsinneed.com/dogshow.

NEUSEY

—— Kathe Traynham, Marketing for a law firm •
Pete Traynham, CBS network television news photographer ——

Pete: A few years ago I was covering a story about a big flood on the Neuse River in North Carolina. Rescue workers had picked up all the people first and were now going back for pets and livestock. The first dog they found was cowering on a porch with the water lapping around her feet. She looked more scared of her rescuers than she was of the flood. They put her in the rescue boat to bring her back to land.

I had the camera on a tripod on a bit of high ground, which was getting smaller by the minute. There was a pretty big crowd gathered around watching—residents who had been flooded out and rescue workers from the sheriff's department and the fire department—probably thirty or forty people. We all watched the dog jump out of the boat. Then this black-and-white, flea-ridden, worm-eaten, skin-and-bones little dog came right over and sat next to me. Next, she put her two front paws up on my leg. She picked me out of the crowd.

Kathe: Really amazing since she was terrified of men and Pete's a pretty big guy, six foot six.

Pete: Anyway she did pick me, so I claim a certain level of innocence here.

Kathe: Pete loves kids, dogs, and old people. If you combine tragedy with any of the above, you never know who or what he will bring home.

Pete: No one there on the bank recognized the dog. She had probably floated down the river and climbed up on that porch. When we finished up work, we piled into the truck, the dog too, for a long five hours on the road trying to get out of there along with everybody else in eastern North Carolina. All the way I was picking fleas and ticks off the dog and throwing them out the window. Finally we arrived at a motel where the office had gotten rooms for us,

but there at the entrance was a huge sign, NO PETS!

I took my duffel up to the room, unpacked it, brought it out to the truck and stuffed the dog in. When we went back inside there was a line at the elevator; the bag was wiggling a little and I was afraid the dog might bark, but she never made a sound.

They decided to put the dog's rescue on that evening's newscast so I called Kathe to tell her to watch it.

"So you're bringing a dog home?"

"Not if you tell me I can't . . ."

Kathe: Yeah, right. It had been eight months since our old dog died, and I was pretty happy with a clean house and less vacuuming, but I guess we were meant to have a dog, especially Pete and especially this dog. So I said, "You better bring her home."

Pete: We decided to name her Neusey after the Neuse River. The first two days of her life with me consisted of one long car trip, being stuffed in and out of suitcases and baths at the motels—nothing but cars and baths. Then when we got home it was off to the vet's for shots and spaying. I think by this time she was having second thoughts about me.

Kathe: We thought it best to get all the bad stuff over right away, so that then her life would just get better and better. She had definitely been abused, and it was much more than just the trauma of the floods. She was very fearful, hated to be picked up, and peed whenever a stranger bent down to pet her. Her dewclaws had been removed with pliers. She was emaciated but wouldn't eat unless she was alone. Fortunately she liked our daughters, but she was particularly scared of men and she still hates little boys.

Pete: Neusey may have picked me first but as soon as she settled down she picked Kathe. She's Kathe's inside dog and my outside dog.

Kathe: We worked hard to socialize her; after a few months she would sleep on her back in my arms. Pete carried her around so much it's a wonder she didn't forget how to walk. She is smart as a whip and desperate to learn and to be of use. In the first two weeks she learned ten tricks, all the tricks we knew. She's just enough border collie to be brilliant, just enough terrier to be fun.

Pete: And Neusey is smart. There is a pile of small car blankets in the corner of our TV room. The dog will grab one, drape it over your foot, and then start chewing on your toes. She knows that it hurts if she chews our bare feet.

Kathe: I had breast cancer six years ago, and for a long time I worried about a lot of things like whether I would see our daughters graduate from high school, then whether I would see them graduate from college. I worried that our thirteen-year-old dog might die while I was having treatments. Then when Neusey showed up, a new dog seemed like a big commitment. As it's turned out, she has been a gift. She is such a happy dog she takes me out of myself and helps me to just enjoy my life.

Anyway, when your husband calls up and says, "This black-and-white, flea-ridden, worm-eaten, skin-and-bones little dog just picked me out of the crowd," what can you do?

HOBBES

—— David Orr, Mortgage broker ——

Years ago when I was living in Boise my roommate, Steve, decided that he wanted a golden retriever. So we went to the pound and met Hobbes. He and his brother had been found on a little island in the Boise River. Both dogs had been severely beaten. They were two years old.

Steve took Hobbes, and a friend of ours took the brother. At first Hobbes was terrified of everything. He was even scared to move. We had to pull him to get him from one room to another. If there were any loud noises like a door slamming he would fall over and start peeing on himself. You couldn't raise a hand anywhere near him. For three months one of us was with him all the time. We gave him a lot of attention and he went to the office with Steve every day. Years passed and Hobbes settled down a lot. All our friends liked him—you can't help it.

Then Steve and Hobbes moved away; they lived in various places and ended up in Newport Beach. Steve found this was not a good place for a dog since they are not allowed on the beach there. It was a really hard decision for Steve but Hobbes came back to live with me. He's been here now for five years.

He's my best buddy. Friends come by my office and pick him up when they're going for a walk, and everyone wants to keep him when I go out of town. He's probably the least loyal dog in the world. He would go off with anyone. He doesn't care much about other dogs but he loves people.

There's no dog who listens better. If you yell at him he'll freak, but if you talk to him in a normal voice, he'll do whatever you ask. One day we were driving in an old van of my dad's when the van caught on fire. I pulled over, opened the door, and screamed at Hobbes to get out. He panicked and shot into the back of the van. So then, with smoke pouring out from under the vehicle, I had to whisper very softly and coax him out. You just can't yell at him, no matter what.

Hobbes is such a good dog. He's actually perfect.

BUSTER, SOPHIE, AND KATO

—— Gayle Morrison, Director of mortgage operations •
Kenneth Bey, The ministry, dry cleaner ——

Gayle: When I was a child I would take steak, cheese, eggs—whatever I could find in my mom's refrigerator—and go out to look for strays. I found quite a few; we had forty-two cats and thirty-one dogs at different times. When I was grown strays continued to find me. Buster, the cocker, came from a coworker who didn't want him. The poor dog lived in a filthy cage all the time. They didn't really like him. When I saw him I knew I couldn't leave him there and Kenny agreed.

I have always taken in strays. Usually I keep them a few weeks, long enough for them to look lovable so someone will adopt them.

Kenneth: At first I wasn't so sure about these dogs Gayle kept finding, but she has taught me compassion.

Gayle: He adjusted. Once we decided to keep Buster, we went to the Humane Society and got Sophie, the beagle, to be a playmate for him.

Then Kato, our Akita, was literally hurled onto our lawn. I was just leaving the house when I heard the car hit him. Minutes later I saw this huge dog staggering across the grass, blood pouring from his mouth. I was scared to touch him so I called the Humane Society, who said they would come over. I had to leave, but when I came home there the dog was on the

deck. I guess he had managed to make it onto the deck and was waiting there for us. Since he was hurt I was worried that he might be mean, but we gave him some water and some food. Then I called the Humane Society again; the dispatcher said that the truck had come out but couldn't take him from our property without permission. Finally they came back and picked him up. They took him first to an emergency clinic where he was treated for chest trauma and a mangled face. When his head was hit he had bitten right through his tongue.

Later he was moved to the shelter, and the next day we went down there to see him. It didn't take me long to see that he was sweet and gentle. Still, so many people said Akitas are likely to be dog-aggressive. I took our two dogs down there to see what the interaction would be. Kato just sniffed them. Actually, in this family it's little Sophie who's the aggressive one. I think there is some Jack Russell in there with the beagle.

Finally it was Kenny who said that we should keep Kato.

Kenneth: Well, you know, I'm in the ministry. I do outreach work through my church, and I guess the love of God has caused me to reach out to animals as well as to people.

INDIE

—— Sue Glasscock, Interior designer ——

Before Indie and I found each other, my husband, Alex, and I lived quite happily with our two cocker spaniels, Chester and Haile. We had absolutely no interest in expanding the family. Then my neighbors rescued a dog and subsequently decided that they couldn't keep it after all. I had heard about Robin Faber, a woman who rescues dogs, so one day I stopped in at Robin's shop to see if she could find a place for the little dog across the street from us. We talked, and when I told her we had two cockers, she said, "Oh, I just rescued this little black cocker. He's at the vet's but he'll be here tomorrow."

Now, Robin had been talking to a homeless woman who lives in her car and rescues dogs. She drives around and tries to find places for them. That day she had twelve dogs in this very small car—eleven pit bulls and pit bull mixes, plus little Indie. The dogs were all tied with ropes and chains and piled on top of each other. Indie had a bad gash on his head. He had been bitten right through the side of his face, perilously close to his eye, which was all milky. His fur was hanging off in patches. He was in pretty bad shape, and Robin felt that she had to take him.

When I came back to the shop the next day, Robin brought out Indie, a scrawny little thing, really skinny, with half his fur missing and this big cut on his poor face. I sat down on the floor; he crawled into my lap and pushed his head under my arm. Alex and I had discussed the possibility of giving the dog a foster home while Robin tried to find a place for him, and when I saw him there was just no question. Besides, I was so impressed with Robin and all

that she has done for these homeless animals that I thought the least I could do was foster this little cocker for a while.

So I took Indie home, and within two days he was like a different dog. I knew almost immediately that we were going to keep him. Alex says he knew when we first talked about fostering that I would never let this dog go. Anyway, it was definitely out of the question.

At first our vet was afraid that Indie might lose the sight in his injured eye but it turned out fine. His face healed up, his coat grew in, and the other dogs eventually accepted him. All our friends bring their dogs over, so Haile and Chester were used to dogs coming to play and then leaving, but this one stayed, and he was getting a lot of attention. Haile, who thinks she's a princess in a dog's body, doesn't really care to interact with other dogs anyway, but Chester loves to play, and now he had a buddy. Slowly over time Indie and Chester became best friends. Now they tear around and have a great time together.

Though he loves Alex, too, Indie is very attached to me. In the first few weeks he tried to follow me everywhere. Once he even jumped out a window to look for me. He's much better now, but when I come home he is always sitting on a chair that looks out over the driveway, staring out the window, waiting for me. To help Indie adjust and feel more comfortable I worked with Cecilia Towner, a dog trainer and animal communicator. I wanted to make him understand that he wasn't going to be abandoned. I think he knows that now but he still likes to keep an eye on me.

Cecilia told me that Indie considers himself my guardian angel, my protector. All I can say is that, before Indie came, I had been having terrible nightmares. Since he has been with us, sleeping as he does with one paw on my chest, one paw next to my head, and his head on my shoulder, I haven't had one bad dream.

Indie is my first rescued dog. My others are spoiled rotten, but Indie is so good—he always comes faster and behaves better. He looks at me as if to say, *Whatever you want, you just name it, and I'll do it if I possibly can!* He's not at all timid. He doesn't seem to have any strange fears or hang-ups. Considering all he's been through, he's remarkably well adjusted. And he is very, very loving—and very demonstrative. We call him Frenchy because he likes to give you a French kiss if you get close enough.

BUDDY

—— *Annie Cowden, Business manager* • *Nancy Kelly, Entrepreneur* ——

Nancy: Seven years ago in the spring a girl-friend and I had a yard sale. A black-and-white dog came by the sale and decided to take a rest under one of the tables. My girlfriend had seen him in her neighborhood early that morning and had put food out for him. She called him Buddy. He was young—probably less than a year old—also starved, scarred, and skittish, pretty beat up with a tear in his neck. We gave him some water; he stayed for a while, then wandered off after a woman with a dog. She took him home and fed him. A little while later he came back and fell asleep under the table.

After the sale my husband, Brian, and I took Buddy to the vet to get his neck sewn up. Then I called Animal Control and the local shelter and put a notice in the paper. Flocks of sheep had been moving through town on their way to summer pasture, and this dog might have run off or been left behind. He was definitely a herding dog, possibly a McNab, which is a kind of cattle dog bred from border collies.

When I brought the dog home from the vet, he was very anxious. I don't think he had ever been in a house before. Everything seemed strange to him, especially the stairs. But at bedtime he followed us up, jumped right on the bed, and cuddled down next to me. That dog is a survivor. When I took him out on a leash, he stayed right tight to my leg. I guess he had figured out that staying near me was a good thing for him.

When no one had claimed him after a while, we had him neutered, hoping that it would make him more adoptable. Brian and I were living in a small condo then; my work schedule was very demanding; we already had a dog, K.C., and we both agreed that we really couldn't have two dogs.

Annie: When Nancy told me the garage sale story, Buddy was there, and even though he was shy, he came right over to me. Nancy explained that she and Brian couldn't keep the dog even though he was so nice. We had a new puppy at my house so I couldn't take him, either, but Stephen, the cook at my restaurant, agreed to try Buddy for a while. Stephen kept him for about a year and then decided to go off to college. He brought Buddy over, saying, "This dog is too nice to go to the pound. Can't you find a home for him?" I called Nancy to tell her that we had Buddy back.

Nancy: I was so happy; I was thrilled. I realized that this was just what I had been hoping for. Stephen had let Buddy run loose in the neighborhood, and I had been worried about him.

As it happened, both our husbands were out of town when Buddy came back, so Annie and I decided that we would each take him part time until we found another home for him. Well, truthfully, neither of us could bear to part with him but we told our husbands we were trying to place him. And we did try—a little.

Annie: We were determined to figure out how we could make it work. Sharing the dog seemed to make sense at the time, and I guess it did make sense because he's been going back and forth between us for five years now. He seems comfortable in both households. It doesn't seem to matter which family he's with. He jumps happily out of one car and into the other. He's just a happy guy.

Nancy: Sharing has been great, a perfect solution that gives each of us time every week to focus on work. This was a way we could keep him. Buddy has rolled with all the changes in his life. It takes him a while to trust people, but he has always been loving with us. He guards

our older dog, K.C., and Annie's dog, Mocha, and us, too, of course. He's alert and protective but not aggressive. He's very gentle with children and loves babies. He goes up to them, gently sniffs them, and gives them the lightest lick. I think he was too much of a softie to work for a sheepherder.

He has a huge heart, and his face is so cute, you have to love him. He does have a good life but he gives us so much more than he gets. And he has given Annie and me a special bonus: We were friends before, although not particularly close friends. Sharing Buddy has made us more like sisters.

LUMPY BEAR

—— *Maurice Tobin, Attorney* ——

When our Samoyed pound dog died, we were desolate. Our daughter, Alexis, decided that we needed a Saint Bernard so she went directly to the Internet and contacted the Saint Bernard Rescue League. Now, the Saint Bernard Rescue League is not a group to call when you are lost in the mountains but an organization that places or "rehomes" Saint Bernards. The computer immediately disgorged the names of sixteen dogs scattered all over the United States. As fate would have it, one was located less than an hour's drive from our house. Alexis and my wife, Joan, were interviewed intensively and extensively by the local Saint Bernard Rescue representative and deemed to be worthy of providing a good home for a Saint Bernard in need. They then drove out to meet the dog and his foster-care provider. Bear was in a horse stall, not an inappropriate venue for a dog who, at three years of age, weighed 185 pounds. Of course he was irresistible.

Joan paid the requisite fees for neutering and shots and gave our telephone number so that the rescue people could call to see if Bear was okay. (There didn't seem to be much interest in whether or not we would be okay.) Bear then climbed into the car, where he occupied the entire backseat and overflowed onto the floor as well. By the time the happy group arrived home he had been rechristened "Lumpy Bear," a name that suits him perfectly.

Bear had been a casualty in a divorce case. Neither the husband nor the wife was willing to give him up to the other, so the judge finally ruled that if they could not agree within a specified time, the dog would go to the Saint Bernard Rescue group. Both were intransigent, and consequently Bear found himself suddenly "available for adoption," as they say in the trade.

Now, three years later, Lumpy Bear's voice shakes our kitchen as he announces arrivals. Buckets of slobber festoon ceilings and walls. No matter how big the car, he takes up most of the space. Nonetheless, he is a wonderful creature, loved not only by us but by all our friends and neighbors and adored by every child he meets.

RUDOLPH

—— Rita Goddard, Retired businesswoman ——

My daughter, Maria, was looking for a dog to be a companion for her friend's mother. She was going out to Hilleary Bogley's shelter, the Middleburg Humane Foundation, and she invited me to go along, so I rode out there with her. We were wandering around looking at all the dogs when Rudolph, this huge guy, part rottweiler, came up to say hello. He got his name because he'd been picked up around Christmas. Well, big old Rudolph took a liking to me for some reason and kind of attached himself to me. Hilleary told us that he had been at the shelter for over a year. She and the others working there just loved him, but I guess people were hesitant to take him home because he is big.

Hilleary, who is also a humane investigator for the state, had taken Rudolph and another dog from a guy who was starving them to death. When the dogs were rescued, Rudolph was about five years old and couldn't stand up. He weighed fifty pounds. His normal weight is 120. The vet wasn't sure if he would survive. He would definitely have been dead if Hilleary had found him even a day or two later.

Maria thought that Rudolph might be good for her friend's mom but she wanted to talk it over with them, so we told Hilleary we would get back to her. A week later Maria decided to try him out for a few days. She called me that morning to ask if she could bring him to our office. I had already told my husband, Rudy, about him, so I told Maria it was okay.

We have always had dogs, but our last dog had died and we hadn't gotten around to even talking about getting another. Rudy had picked up that dog on the highway in a snowstorm on his way home from work, and when he brought the puppy into the house, he said, "Remember, we are not keeping this dog." We did try to find the owner, with no luck, but he was a good little dog so we ended up keeping him. For eighteen years he was my bosom buddy. When he went, it was really hard—both of us crying around here.

Anyway, Maria brought Rudolph over, and my husband flipped out over him, too. We've had him ever since. He moved in and kind of took over. He decided right away he needed the sofa in the family room to sleep on, and it's still his bed today. I finally bought another sofa for us.

Rudolph is so mellow and laid back; he was especially perfect for our situation. Rudy had Parkinson's disease. Sometimes he was depressed, but he would go out anyway and walk the dog or play with him in the house. He was more attached to this dog than to any other we had ever had. He used to say, "That dog must be in my life for a reason." It is amazing that such a good dog would stay at the shelter for a whole year. Who knows—maybe he was waiting for us. He fit into our lives so perfectly.

At times my husband wasn't able to get around very well so I had to help him a lot. But Rudolph didn't demand anything of us. He was just happy to be there. It's strange that he could be so sweet, considering everything that had happened to him. We thought maybe he had been with someone who really loved him when

he was young, and then somehow he fell into bad hands.

But the dog has had an easy life since he's been here. In the mornings he sleeps in if he wants to. He eats and naps and goes out in the backyard to chase squirrels when he feels like it. He loves it when the grandchildren come over to visit. He and I take our walk every day and talk to each other a little bit now and then. We have become even closer since Rudy died. I'm awfully glad he's here, especially now that I'm by myself.

Rudy used to say, "The first thing that dog took was my name, the second thing he took was my sofa in the family room." I guess the third thing he took was our hearts.

HATTIE CAKES

—— Fran Jewell, Dog trainer ——

One day about five years ago my friends Bob and Sue called me about an eight-month-old black-and-silver German shepherd who needed a home. They knew I was a soft touch for dogs, especially shepherds. The owners had said they were moving the next day and couldn't take her along. We learned later that they had simply left their cats at the house when they took off. They probably would have done the same with Hattie if Bob and Sue had not agreed to find a place for her. I thought it over for three days and then took her home with me.

Hattie's young couple had gotten her when she was a puppy. A few months later they had a baby and Hattie was banished to the backyard. This scenario seems to be quite common: People who are feeling a nesting urge go out and get a dog; then they have a baby and no time for the poor dog. Ask anyone who works in a shelter.

Anyway, Hattie certainly had been neglected. They called her "Pain." That was her name. She looked at water in a bowl as if she had no idea what it was. She didn't know how to play; balls and toys meant nothing to her. She didn't know *sit* or *come*. She didn't know what to make of other dogs. She wasn't afraid of them; she just didn't know what to do with them.

As soon as I started to work with Hattie, I began to realize how incredible she is, what a great potential she has. She is extremely intelligent and very willing. She also has a wonderful personality. She is the most affectionate of all the dogs I've ever had. She doesn't just sit next to you—she leans against you and snuggles up. She is the epitome of the loyal, loving, tolerant German shepherd.

Hattie's wonderful temperament made her a good 4-H dog for my daughter, Jessica. I began training her in obedience and search and rescue. After three months with us Hattie had earned her American Kennel Club (AKC) Companion Dog title for obedience and a Delta Society certification for pet therapy.

The first time I took her to visit at our local nursing home we met a man called Marlon who loved dogs. Hattie jumped right up on the bench beside him and put her head on his shoulder. I will never forget the look of delight on Marlon's face. It seemed as if Hattie knew that this was a nice old man who would love some special attention from her. Watching them together brought such joy to my heart.

Last year Hattie won a National Special Services award from Delta; she was one of only forty-four nominees nationwide for the AKC pet therapy ACE award. She has earned two legs on a Novice Agility title. She participates in Blaine County Search and Rescue. In addition to all this, she is vice president in charge of demonstration and socialization for my business, Positive Puppy Dog Training.

Hattie is no "Pain" to me!

McCOY

—— *Lisa Mullins Thompson, Retail store owner* ——

When I first started my shop, I worked by myself all day. I had come from the State Department, where I was accustomed to being around lots of people, lots of activity. My husband, Damon, and I thought maybe I should get a dog, partly for security, but mainly for company. Then we thought about liability issues and what kind of dog I could actually have in the store—certainly one who was friendly and mellow. We both like to sail and we wanted a dog who liked the water so we could take it on the boat with us. The solution seemed obvious—a Labrador! Labs love people, children, and water; also they're big enough to offer protection.

I had never had a dog so I wasn't quite sure where to begin, but one of my friends who has worked with dogs recommended that we not get a puppy for a variety of reasons—housebreaking, chewing, and all that wild puppy energy. So we called Labrador Retriever Rescue. After a rigorous screening that included references, an interview, and visits to our home and to the store as well, we were finally approved as a potential home for a needy Labrador. We were on the list.

One day Susan Wells, who ran the rescue league, called to say, "Someone has just brought your dog here. This is the perfect match!" Of course we went right out to see this dog, and there was McCoy. It *did* seem like the perfect match. But I was about to leave on a two-week buying trip in Europe so Susan agreed to keep the dog to give him a smooth transition when we returned.

The night we came home from the trip Damon and I went out to Susan's house to pick up McCoy. After greeting him I started signing all the papers. Susan, who wanted us to understand the seriousness of helping the dog make a good start in his new life, warned us that he might be nervous in a new place, that it might be better not to take him to the store for a week or two, that he might lift his leg everywhere at first. I hesitated. "I don't know about this," I said. I started to put down the papers. Then McCoy nudged my arm quite firmly with his nose. *Come on, come on, let's get this over with,* he seemed to say. *I want to go home.* What could I do? I finished signing the adoption papers.

When we arrived home McCoy walked from room to room, sniffed everywhere, and then lay down right where he is now. The next day I decided to try him at the store. It was the same thing: He walked around, sniffed around, and then plopped down. It was so easy. It was just as if he knew he was in a safe place where people were going to love him.

McCoy has become a great conversation piece at the store. He's so great looking and always friendly, calm, and gentle. People come into the store saying, "Where did you get him? Where did you get him?" Then they call Labrador Rescue and say, "I've met McCoy and I want a dog just like him." Some customers bring their children in just to see him.

From the time they were puppies, McCoy and his brother had lived with a family in the D.C. area. The dogs lived in the house and were part of the family. Then these people built a new house out in the country on the water, and after they moved in the wife decided that she didn't like the idea of two big wet dogs in her new

house. So the dogs were relegated to the garage at night and tied up outside on a line all day with an endless supply of free-choice food. Needless to say, they gained weight. Soon they were 125 pounds—obese, lethargic, and depressed. After about six months of this, I guess the owners realized that it was not a good life for the two dogs and called Labrador Rescue. It certainly turned out to be a good thing for me.

I had no idea a dog could have so much personality. He loves to be petted; he loves attention. Sometimes I think he knows that he has landed on his feet because he seems so appreciative. His tail is always wagging—when he eats, when he drinks, when he goes to greet a customer coming in the door. People say, "That is the happiest dog I have ever seen." And I'm the happiest shopkeeper, thanks to my canine business partner.

GIZMO

—— Mary Dayle McCormick, Bookstore manager ——

No more pets!"
I was adamant. With two teenagers, a husband, two big dogs, three cats, a pond full of goldfish, my job, and a fresh diagnosis of multiple sclerosis, another responsibility was the last thing I needed. Or so I thought.

One bright autumn morning when I had been having a particularly difficult time managing the MS symptoms, my husband returned home from the bookstore to check on me. When I greeted him at the door, he pointed to his feet, saying, "What's this?"

I looked down. A dark ball of fur with huge eyes and a long silky tail returned my gaze as if to say, *Here I am.* Then the creature stood on her hind legs, grinning, tail twirling, floppy ears flipped up like Gizmo the Gremlin. For my husband it was love at first sight, but for me it was still, "No more pets!"

Following the proper found-pet protocol, we called the animal shelter to pick up the dog. We then posted notes at all the area vet offices.

Still, I was haunted by the thought of the adorable little thing being euthanized at the end of a three-day waiting period. I called twice each day to ask if she had been claimed. The news was not reassuring. So of course, seventy-two hours and four minutes after the shelter picked her up, the dog became ours. That was eight years ago and I can't remember what life was like without Gizmo.

She has been a true godsend. Sure, she's another muzzle to feed, another vet bill to pay. But her constant companionship and gentle, sunny disposition have nursed me through dark days. Whether she's with me at the bookstore greeting customers, riding along in the basket of my scooter, or snuggled in my lap, pain and uncertainty seem less ominous when Gizmo is there. With her, quiet times are more restful, solitude less lonely. And she's a hoot when I scratch her tickle spot.

Evidently, another responsibility was just what I needed.

HOSS

—— *Josiah Whitaker, Veterinary assistant* ——

Yes, Hoss was rescued. My wife, Cindy, is a big softie like me when it comes to the dogs, and she found him one day running along the highway. He was full grown but young, part shepherd, part something else. People at the shelter told us that he had been turned in twice as a stray, each time redeemed by his owners who must have gotten tired of this because they had passed him on to a friend who made no effort to keep Hoss safe or to look for him when he disappeared. When the original owners learned that we had found the dog, they told us we could have him.

My wife and I already had two dogs. We weren't looking for a third, but we never have been able to turn a blind eye to a stray. During the past six years we have found homes for at least a dozen strays and this was our intention for Hoss. After about six months we did find what seemed to be a good home, but it didn't work out and soon Hoss was back at our house. We decided that he was with us to stay.

First we did some obedience work. Then I decided to have him certified as a Delta Society Pet Partner for Animal Assisted Therapy (AAT). Shep, my Lab mix, had been working in a program for kids who were in trouble with the law but not actually in detention, and I thought Hoss could be an understudy. Well, the understudy became the star. While Shep had been kind and patient with the kids and tolerated them pretty well, Hoss actually enjoyed them! Watching him with these kids and their unpredictable behavior, I realized that he could work with a more demanding population, so we started in an early-intervention program with autistic children.

Later Hoss and I became one of the first six teams ever certified with HOPE Crisis Response

AAT. Crisis-response dogs must be able to cope with challenging levels of stress, with sirens, smoke, screaming, heavy equipment, subway and air travel, long hours, and heavy emotions. Hoss is particularly good in these situations for one main reason: He adapts. He looks around, and then no matter what he sees, he seems to say, *Oh, so this is what's going on. Okay.* Hoss was the first canine to work on the Oregon Crisis Response Team, which responds to traumatic events likes plane crashes and fires, plus all kinds of natural disasters. We were part of the team that responded to the school shooting at Thurston High School in 1998. Hoss was one of the first two dogs to work under the Red Cross in times of disaster.

After September 11, Hoss and a keeshond called Tikva were the two dogs who first opened up Ground Zero to selected AAT teams. Tikva's handler, Cindy Ahlers from HOPE, and I flew in from Portland with the dogs to help mental health counselors at the site in their efforts to reach out to traumatized workers and later at the Family Assistance Center. In New York we worked twelve-hour days for ten days; we just couldn't stop, because we knew our time was limited. Even when we were taking a break, people kept coming up to the dogs, so *they* never really had a break.

But every day we saw people turning to the dogs. The ultimate goal in crisis-response work is to help people who have experienced trauma begin talking about their experiences with a professional who can help them process the event in a healthy and healing way. One family seemed to identify Hoss with their son, another looked at him as a kind of guide to the next world, others simply turned away from the view of Ground Zero and buried their faces in the

dog's fur. It seemed as if the dogs made this horrible time a little easier.

It was the first time I ever saw Hoss tired. He does so well with stress, but I can see when he starts dragging; the tail is a great indicator. When we finally came home, we were both drained, but especially Hoss. In New York he didn't want to sleep—he wanted to work—but once back home he slept twenty hours or more every day for a month. I began to think about my dog and the stress he appears to manage so easily. It seemed as if just a little of his spark was gone. I had asked so much of him in New York,

but I don't ever want to push him. I think he's done enough. There are many good teams in HOPE so Hoss is retiring now.

We still work with the autistic children, and that's plenty challenging. Even though I watch the dog like a hawk he still gets poked in the eye and stepped on more than I would like. He's always understanding and forgiving.

Hoss deserves the credit for all of his accomplishments. I'm like a parent who drives a gifted child across town every day to exercise a creative gift or talent. We are a team but Hoss is the star of the show. That dog has a solid heart of gold.

LUCKY DIAMOND

—— Wendy Diamond, Publisher of Animal Fair ——

WARNING: BEWARE OF DOG! That's what it says in the FedEx deliveryman's notes on our office address. My dog, Lucky, is a four-pound Maltese. She is also a self-appointed guard dog, and she takes her job very seriously. When the buzzer rings, whether for FedEx or pizza delivery, she hurls herself at the door, sometimes jumping as high as four feet in the air, barking and growling ferociously.

Her previous owner couldn't handle the fact that she's so hyperactive. I take her everywhere with me, partly because I love her, but partly because she has abandonment issues and she has trained me to accommodate them. In a bag she's quiet; she just goes to sleep. I have a million little bags.

She's still wildly hyperactive, but you know what? If your dog has a problem, you can't just give it away.

SOPHIE

—— Elizabeth Peters, Sophie's companion ——

When I first went looking for a dog in New York City I was accompanied by our daughter, Rachel, a stern taskmaster. I saw a cute dog at the ASPCA but Rachel said, "You can't take that one. She's adorable. Anyone would take her. You should find one who really needs you."

Obediently, I agreed to go to the city Animal Control facility, where there were certainly lots of dogs who needed someone, but they were all large dogs. Some of them looked ferocious, and I didn't think I could handle them. You feel horrible going away from those places empty-handed, but I was determined to find the right dog.

When Daisy, our old dog, came up the path years ago and decided to adopt Alton, my husband, I didn't know much about dogs and their behavior. Daisy and I never really clicked, which was fine with Daisy, who adored Alton and only Alton. This time I wanted a dog I could really love.

I mustered my courage and told Rachel that I thought we should go back to the ASPCA and the dog who had appealed to me in the first place. There was Sophie, waiting for us. She was about a year old, lively, and she seemed very normal. She looked like a lovable dog. They let her out of the cage. She raced around, obviously thrilled to be free. She did not seem at all traumatized. There was something about her that appealed to me. After all the rational evaluation, one day a dog just appeals to you, and you take her home.

At first I took Sophie out every two hours, kept the closets closed, and put things I didn't want chewed out of reach. Gradually I began to realize that she was not only well behaved but housebroken as well. She just seemed happy to do the right thing. She had been picked up as a stray in Brooklyn, this wonderful dog. She must have been lost. Someone had certainly loved her and worked with her. I wish I knew her story, but I probably never will.

Before I got Sophie I did some research, read books, and talked to many dog lovers. I realized that a dog is a real commitment, and I wanted to be able to love one. This is the first time in my life that I have felt really committed to a dog. I think it only happens when you put in a great deal of effort. Sophie absorbs a huge amount of affection and sends it back again to me.

STELLA

—— *Elise Galpin, Fund-raiser for nonprofit literacy organization* ——

When a ranch south of here went on the market, the realtors showing the property found Stella with a litter of puppies, plus several other dogs, all locked in a stall in the barn. They were horrified at the state of these dogs; the poor things were filthy, mangy and starving, and they certainly did not enhance the look of the ranch. The owner said, "I don't care what you do with those animals. Just get them out of here."

So the dogs went off to the pound. The puppies were adopted right away. They were gone by the time I got there so I never saw them. I took some other dogs, one at a time, out into the yard to play, winnowed the selection down to two finalists, and took them each for a walk. They were both nice dogs but neither one really moved me.

There was another dog all by herself in a pen, and it turned out to be the mother of the pups from the ranch. Her name was Stella.

We went out for a walk and I liked her immediately. For starters, she was beautiful, but I was really drawn to her personality. Not being at all impulsive, however, I knew I had to wait and come back another day to reassess.

The next morning I was back at the shelter when it opened. Stella and I set off on a long walk up in the hills behind the shelter. She seemed independent, not at all timid. She would range ahead looking for squirrels and gophers, but always checking back to see where I was.

By the time we got back to the shelter I had decided that Stella was the dog for me, and she seemed to agree, so I brought her home.

In the beginning we (and especially my husband, Amos) had to be very careful about reaching for anything that could be considered a weapon—like a flyswatter, for instance. If Amos picked up the flyswatter, Stella would run upstairs and hide under the bed.

Shortly after I adopted her we started to work with Fran Jewell, a great dog trainer who immediately pointed out that Stella was highly motivated by food. I had a smart dog who would do anything for a treat, a perfect candidate for obedience training. Well, we did obedience training, and we did a lot of it. Eventually we even entered an obedience competition. We went through all the competition routines many times at home and Stella was perfect, so we went off to the show with great expectations. The first day my star was eliminated for "fouling the ring"—extremely embarrassing, but I suppose she just thought she was marking a new territory. The next day she did *not* foul the ring, but she didn't do anything else either—no sit, no stay, no heel, nothing. It just wasn't her cup of tea. She loved class; class was fun, and there were treats. There were no treats in the show ring. That was our one and only show.

When I first got Stella, my mom gave me a book called *Culture Clash*, by Jean Donaldson; this book completely changed the way I thought about dogs. It gave me an understanding about how things seem from the dog's perspective, and it helped me structure my training and learn to frame what I was asking Stella to do in ways that made sense to her. I learned how to make it easy for her to be a good dog. I give *Culture Clash* (and Mom) a lot of the credit for the great dog Stella has become.

Stella loves to play. A sprinkler is her idea of a

perfectly wonderful toy. When we first started hiking together, she initiated a favorite game. She likes to get ahead of me, preferably slightly uphill. She crouches down on her belly, as flat as she can. Then when I get close, she bursts forward and jumps on me. I have to shriek and act startled, and she races off thoroughly pleased with herself.

I certainly get much more exercise with Stella's encouragement. She loves exercise—in fact she requires it—so we go cross-country skiing all winter and running in the hills the rest of the year. If I'm busy in the office or around the house, she

will give me just so much slack. Then she says, *It's time to go do something!* She is very expressive and persuasive for a creature who doesn't use words.

She's great company, and is always happy to see me. Amos says the thing he likes most about her is the happiness she gives me. She does make me happy, and she makes me smile, sometimes even laugh out loud. I have to strive to live up to all this devotion. As the saying goes, "Try to be the person your dog thinks you are." Stella is a remarkable dog, even if she hasn't rescued any children from canals. She's just a sweetie.

PRECIOUS

—— Tanya Nielsen, Real estate development ——

A few months ago my friend Robin, who rescues dogs, picked up a little brown terrier mix on a busy street. As cars whizzed by, the dog was walking along in the gutter bumping into the curb from time to time. She was about thirteen, pitifully thin, blind and deaf. Shortly after that I happened to see Robin, and I said to her, "I've been thinking about getting a dog. If you ever have an old blind dog, a small one, maybe even deaf, give me a call."

Robin looked amazed, but my request was not as crazy as it sounds. I used to have a blind cocker spaniel, Dudley, and he had been very easy and mellow. I work long days and have two cats, also known as the Kittens. I didn't want to upset them, and I didn't have the time to exercise and entertain an energetic young dog. Besides, I love old people and old animals.

Well, Robin immediately whipped out pictures of Precious, this sweet little brown terrier. As soon as I saw her I knew that I had to have her. There was one hurdle: I already had two rescued dogs, a shepherd and a springer who were living with my parents in the country. I think you could say that my parents are unwilling but loving rescuers. Anyway, they had told me that if I ever even thought about getting a dog, I would have to take one of the two they were keeping for me. Precious and I had to persuade them, and especially Dad, that she needed to stay with me. When I took her to meet them, it was as if she knew that my dad was the one she had to win over. She walked right up to him and when he picked her up she just snuggled up under his chin. "Why," he said. "she looks just like Muffin." Muffin was a dog Dad had rescued and loved many years earlier so I knew everything would be fine.

Precious had one problem: She seemed to have forgotten everything about housebreaking. She just went everywhere, and, worse still, she usually walked in it. I called Best Friends Sanctuary to ask about training an old, blind, deaf dog. Their first response was, "Are you sure you want to do this?" Well, of course I was sure.

It really wasn't too bad, especially after she got over the *Giardia*. She was really, really sick, with vomiting and terrible diarrhea. She dropped from eleven to eight pounds in almost no time, and I had to rush her over to the emergency care for IV fluids and nutrients. Now she's totally fine. She's even getting a little Buddha belly.

On the housebreaking front, I think she mainly needed a routine. I would set the alarm for 5 A.M. so that I was sure to wake up before she did. Then I would take her right out. I got a dog walker for the middle of the day, and then I was home in the evening. As soon as she became accustomed to the routine it seemed as if things started to come back to her, things like *outside is the place to go to the bathroom*. She still has accidents sometimes, especially if I get home a little late, but now they're near the door.

Maybe the previous owners dumped her when she got sick. I guess people can get tired of an old, blind, deaf dog, especially one with *Giardia*.

But everything's fine now. In just a few months this little dog has fit in here so well. *Precious* is a perfect name for her. The Kittens

think she's great. They like to stalk her and then they whiz by like hummingbirds—actually more like fighter jets. Precious doesn't seem to mind. The dog walker loves her. He's a big guy, six foot six, and as you can imagine, they're quite a pair. This little dog is very calming for me. My work is pretty high stress, but when I come home at night and take Precious out for a walk, everything slows down, way down. In fact she walks so slowly that I often wear a headlamp and read the paper while we meander along. When I pick her up she just melts under my chin. She's my girl.

Of course Precious is lucky—lucky that Robin found her, lucky to be here with me now—but she gives me so much more than I give her. I'm really the lucky one, just so lucky that she came into my life.

FLEA, OLIVER, AND AGNES

—— *Kathryn Walker, Theatrical director* ——

When I found Flea I was on location in Virginia acting in a TV movie with Jack Lemmon. We were filming at this beautiful old Federal house surrounded by slums that had encroached right up to the fence. Just outside that fence was the craft services truck supplying eggs, bacon, and burritos for actors and crew. Of course, this vehicle smelled like every stray's dream, so naturally all the starving animals in the neighborhood were there. In the midst of them was Flea, about six months old. She was tiny, maybe twice the size of a Chihuahua. I noticed her out of the corner of my eye. Two large tough cats were hissing and snarling at her, trying to drive her away from the food.

Throughout the morning I kept seeing her. Finally I couldn't stand it any longer, so I marched over to the fence and started asking bystanders if anyone knew who this dog belonged to, and nobody did. When I said that I would like to buy her, suddenly everyone owned her. At that point I had to go and get dressed for a ballroom scene. Fortunately, there was a nice assistant producer who continued the negotiations for me through the fence. Between takes I kept running out in my satin ball gown to see what was happening. At the end of the day the producer had managed to get Flea for forty dollars. I found her on the porch in a cardboard box with a little rope noose around her neck.

I took Flea back to the hotel where she was admired by everyone. Room service sent up some pieces of leftover steak for her dinner; she had a bath and went to sleep on my bed. The next morning, after I had taken her to the vet for shots and a collar and leash, we went back to work. Our first stop was the makeup truck. I sat down with the dog on my lap, but as soon as the makeup person came near me Flea started to growl. And it was like that for the next fifteen years—I was her personal property. Nell—I sometimes called her Nell as a term of endearment—took over my life; we were inseparable. She was the most extraordinary dog and a published poet besides. There is a poem of hers, with a self-portrait of us, in the book, *Unleashed.*

There will never be another Nell, and when she died I was in despair. After a while a friend said to me, "I think it's time to take some baby steps here." She started calling around to various pounds to look for little dogs. Then she found an ad for a three-month-old rat terrier, so we went to see Oliver, who was living in a tiny apartment with small children and people who worked all day. It was a crazy situation, and I took him even though I had never had a terrier and never had a male dog before. Oliver is an adorable guy, lovable and adorable, but he *is* a guy, so it's about chasing the ball, it's about eating, and he certainly doesn't want to talk about the relationship.

Funny and sweet as Oliver was, I still felt a longing for that little Chihuahua face—actually a little Chihuahua mix—in my life again. I started looking on the Internet. Then I had some great conversations with Katherine Schlintz and Kaye La Rocque at the PAL Humane Society, located in a tough, rural area in California that seems to be the Chihuahua-mix capital of America. There are people there who obtain dogs from free-to-a-good-home ads and then eat them or sell them to people who do. There are people who take dogs from the same free-to-a-good-home ads, then tie them to trees and train pit bulls to kill them. The saints who run PAL are really up against it. I am so impressed by them, but I

don't know how they can keep going when they witness so much suffering.

In the meantime I went to Los Angeles for Thanksgiving, and while I was there I got in touch with a Doberman rescue group in Fillmore that had an adjunct called Little Paws.

Then, six weeks later, on my birthday, Ardis Munck from Fillmore called to say that she had a dog for me. One of her scouts had found a little Chihuahua mix through PAL. In the photograph on the computer this dog really didn't look much like Nell, but with all the synchronicity—my birthday and the dog coming from the people I admired so much at PAL—I couldn't say no. It seemed as if everything was saying, *Do it!*

So I did it. I adopted Agnes. When she arrived she was shaking all over, terrified, but within forty-five minutes she and Oliver were madly chasing each other. Agnes is a little white Chihuahua mix with fawn markings around her ears. She's ravishingly beautiful. When you see her, you can just imagine the tiny tiara that should be on the top of her head. She looks like a little princess, but she's not. She's actually quite a hard case, very needy, wary, and defensive.

I have only had her with me for a few weeks, but I can see already that as she gets more confident she is going to be a wonderful dog. There is this defensiveness about her now, but after all, she's little, and she's afraid. She has a terrible fear of men but she likes women—actually, to be perfectly honest, at the moment she really doesn't like anyone but me. She's glued to me; I think it will give her confidence in the long run, and I know she will be fine. It's going to be fascinating to watch this little dog emerge. I can't wait to really know her.

I love Oliver madly but I'm so happy to have a girl again. It's a whole different thing. Agnes has a kind of subtlety, and she's a little thief, which I love. She climbs up on tables, just the way Nell did, and steals stuff—food or things she wants to chew. I love that resourcefulness.

Doberman Pinscher and Little Paws Rescue, 2946 Young Road, Fillmore, CA 93015; www.dobierescue@earthlink.net.
PAL Humane Society, 16044 Bear Valley Road, Victorville, CA 92392; www.palhs.org.

HIGHWAY HARRY

—— Joan Baker, Photographer ——

As I was driving along with some friends one evening at dusk we spotted a little black thing on the side of the road. When we stopped to investigate we discovered a tiny puppy, probably no more than two weeks old, crouched by the side of the road shaking to bits. I was the first one out of the car. I knew right away that he was my dog.

Highway Harry grew up strong and healthy and very handsome. For years he would not go near a car. When I moved I had a tranquilizer to give him, but I didn't have to use it. When he saw my car piled to the ceiling with stuff, he managed to wedge himself in somehow and off we went to the new house. He didn't want to be left behind.

I think he knows that he was saved, and I must admit that once in a while I remind him.

Harry is a noble dog with a great personality and much dignity. In my photographs it is engagement and connection that interest me. Harry is definitely engaged in my life. We have a real connection. He gives me a feeling of well-being; I hope I do the same for him.

GEORGIA LOUISE

—— Kari Isaksen, Paper store manager and buyer ——

For years I had begged my parents for a dog, but they always said, "Wait until you have your own place."

When I finished school I was still living at home and still longing for a dog. One day a friend suggested going to some dog pounds just to look. I said, "We can't do that," but after a little more discussion, we set out. We ended up in a pretty depressing place and there, in a cage at the very end of a long hall, was Georgia—gangly and cute and only three months old. When we took her out she was incredibly calm. I thought, *Oh no, I've actually found a dog! Now what will I do?*

I took her back to the store where I was working and then eventually home to my parents' house. When Mom came in she had already heard about Georgia from my sister, and she was not pleased. "I just can't believe you simply went out and got a dog," she said.

Then Dad arrived. He was in the kitchen when Georgia came barreling down the hall. He got this big grin on his face, and the only thing he said was, "Are we keeping her?" Both of my parents fell in love with the dog immediately. It was lucky that she was sweet and well behaved. From that day on Georgia became my best friend and companion. She has a very special disposition. Even as a three-month-old puppy she was remarkably mellow.

We went to dog-training classes, both puppy and novice, and I hired a trainer to come to the store to help get her established there. In four years she has never missed a day of work. Customers seem to be drawn to her. Every week there are people who come in especially to see her. Sometimes they bring their kids.

Georgia likes the store, but she loves the weekends. She likes to go out for breakfast. We always choose an outdoor café where she can sleep under the table. Sometimes we do errands, and then, her favorite thing, we go sailing. She loves the boat and the water in general. She will happily spend hours at the beach splashing around and retrieving an old sandal.

She does have a pretty good life. Actually both of us are very, very lucky.

HOUDINI

—— *Mazie Blanks, Physician recruiter* ——

While vacationing on the Greek island of Santorini, I found a stray bearded collie rummaging through the garbage. There was no doubt in my mind that the dog was 100 percent beardie. I had three bearded collies of my own back home in Atlanta, and I know and love the breed. This dog was small for an adult male, and he looked as if he had never had a bath or seen a brush, but his temperament was all beardie: sweet, loving, and quite untouched by his tough life as a stray. The dog followed me around all day and seemed delighted that a friendly visitor had come his way. The market had no dog food, so I went to a restaurant and bought food for all the stray dogs in the neighborhood. We had a street party!

The next day I returned with a collar and leash, caught the bearded collie, and loaded him, with some difficulty, into my car. Then I drove the dog, who was more than a little scared and confused, to a veterinarian, Dr. Margarita Valvis-Roussou. Truly an Angel of Mercy, she has set up a shelter for strays where they get food and health care until homes can be found for them. Strays are a real problem for the residents of Santorini. Many visitors bring dogs with them when they come to the island for a vacation, and then abandon the animals when they depart. There are not enough homes for all these strays, and since most are not neutered, the population keeps expanding. Many are killed by the Animal Control authorities, but Dr. Valvis-Roussou saves as many as she can, sending a number of them to a shelter in Germany where they have a better chance of being adopted.

When we arrived, the shelter staff examined the dog. He was malnourished and very thin; he had cataracts on both eyes. I named him Houdini because I was determined that he would escape his old life as a stray. I discovered later that he had been rescued before, escaped from the shelter, and made his way through the mountains back to the town where I later found him. Clearly *Houdini* was an appropriate name.

When I returned to Atlanta I set up a Houdini home page on the Internet. To my amazement there were thousands of hits on this page from all over the world. In less than two days, Gottfried and Margot Klein-Konradt, a couple from Germany, had offered to adopt him. Houdini was flown to Germany, where he met his new owners as well as several newspaper reporters and a reporter from the local radio station. The rescue had involved people in three countries and three different languages. Houdini was certainly a very lucky dog, and he was famous!

He wagged his tail and greeted everyone warmly. Then, although his legs were still a little unsteady from the flight, he climbed up on the sofa next to Margot and Gottfried without any shyness and laid his head on their laps. He had come home. He was their dog.

Eight months later I visited the family in Germany. Houdini was obviously very happy. With a healthy diet and medical treatment his cataracts have completely disappeared. Margot and Gottfried (and their grandchildren) get a lot of pleasure with him, and also a lot of exercise. They told me it was love at first sight, and I think Houdini would agree. This dog I found eating garbage now lives near the Black Forest and rides around in a Mercedes. I wish someone would rescue me!

VINNIE

—— Doris Kohls, Veterinary technician, animal shelter staff member ——

I was working at our local animal shelter two days before Christmas when a three-month-old rottweiler puppy arrived in a box. A nice man had discovered the puppy, unable to stand or walk, under his parked car in the Bronx. At first we thought the dog might be weak from parvo so we took him to the vet. The dog had no apparent injuries except broken blood vessels in the whites of his eyes. An X ray, however, showed considerable cervical damage. The vet thought that someone had tried unsuccessfully to hang the puppy and then dumped him on the street. There was no way of knowing whether he would ever walk.

On Christmas Day I went into the shelter to feed the animals, and there was the poor thing just lying there but so happy to see me, the little tail trying to wag. I couldn't bear to leave him, so I took him to my sister's for dinner. Since he couldn't walk I figured he wouldn't cause any trouble. That day I named him Vinnie and I knew he was mine. My husband and I already had three unadoptable dogs, so he wasn't particularly surprised by the new addition. Vinnie joined Jack, a bottle baby, Tyler who had psychological problems probably relating to his life with a drug addict, and Duffer who had been dropped and walks with a tilt.

At first I used an extended harness on Vinnie to help him stand. If I held him he could even goose-step a little with straight legs. He dragged himself around to play with the other dogs. He always seemed happy and he was very sweet, never afraid of people. Little by little he began to haul himself up and take a few steps on his own before collapsing. He couldn't make turns at all. Now he can walk, though not exactly like a normal dog. He picks his feet up very high. He can go up the stairs but not down.

Vinnie is my first rottweiler. I'm actually an Irish setter girl so I want the dog to think he's an Irish setter. He has always been very social. He often comes to the shelter to play with the dogs there. Vinnie's social skills more than compensate for his motor skills. He throws his whole body into wagging.

SMOKEY

—— Shalott Hazzard, Special education teacher ——

One day last April I was driving by an empty lot, one that I pass every day on my way to work. I saw a puppy on the side of the road, and I said to myself, *I'm not going to stop. I am definitely not going to stop!* After about a block I turned around and went back. The puppy was right there where I had first seen him. He was probably about six weeks old and so little that I could hold him in one hand. He was the funniest, cutest thing you ever saw.

I took him to school with me that day and every day after that for the next three months. My students, kindergartners to fifth-graders, all loved him. Even now, kids come up to me and say, "Where's Smokey?" Once in a while, I take him in to visit.

Sometimes as a puppy, Smokey was a real pain. His chewing phase was endless. He chewed everything—socks, chair legs, my ankles, my fingers—chew, chew, chew. He didn't discriminate.

Now that he's theoretically an adult, he is still the cutest, funniest thing. Even my husband, Jalal, who's not so sure about this dog rescue business, will admit that Smokey's cute. I think the dog is part pit bull, part English bulldog. He looks as if he's wearing a jacket with sleeves a little too short. And that tongue . . . It's partly paralyzed so it hangs out of one side of his mouth. If you don't want to be licked, you have to stay on his other side. He makes these funny, snorty, slurpy noises all the time. He's a little snorty pig.

Every morning he sits at the top of the stairs and waits for me. He needs his hug before he goes downstairs. Don't try this at home—many dogs *HATE* to be hugged. It scares them.

Smokey likes to play with our two cats. It's a game for all of them. When he was a puppy they scratched him a few times, so he has a lot of respect for them. I have an old dog recuperating in the garage now. His name is Zachary, and he was in pretty bad shape when I picked him up. Smokey is crazy about Zachary, and they play a little, but Zachary gets sick of him pretty quickly.

Everyone who sees Smokey loves him. I just got him an agent. My sister-in-law took some pictures for his head shot. Who knows? Maybe Hollywood is right around the corner.

I just love this dog. Every day I'm grateful that I have him. He's always happy, and that makes me happy.

CODY

—— *Eric Schoenberg, Prosecutor* • *Elizabeth Schoenberg, Investment adviser* ——

My wife, Elizabeth, and I definitely wanted a dog. Someday. We had each grown up in homes filled with dogs, and we knew that dogs would be a part of our own home. Someday. At the time we lived in an apartment and were both working, so it just wasn't practical. Fortunately, fate overruled our sensible plans.

One afternoon, in the middle of a heat wave, I was walking home from the train station when I saw a very strange scene. A car was stopped in the middle of a small side street, the engine running and both front doors open. Two women were hovering over something on the ground under a tree. I joined them and saw a dirty, emaciated, semiconscious dog wrapped in a blanket. At first I thought that the dog had been hit by the car, but one of the women, Nancy Harmon, explained that he had been tied to the tree all day, apparently abandoned. She said that she was willing to take him to a vet, but if he survived, which seemed unlikely, she couldn't keep him. I explained that my wife and I couldn't take him in, either, but for some reason I then proceeded to give her our phone number. When I lifted the poor dog into Nancy's car he seemed so light, probably less than twenty-five pounds, and he did not move at all. There was a pool of blood on the ground where he had been lying.

I went home and told Elizabeth about what had happened. We talked for a long time about the fact that it was not only impractical but virtually impossible for us to adopt a dog at that point in our lives.

A few days later we heard that the dog was going to survive but that there was no hope of a home for him. He had a serious case of parvovirus and would remain contagious to other dogs for several weeks. Consequently, no animal shelter could take him. My wife and I continued to hem and haw for a while, but we knew that if we did not take him the dog would be "put to sleep." On the other hand, we knew nothing about this dog. Elizabeth had never even seen him. The dog could be friendly or vicious, housebroken or not; there was simply no way of knowing. So we called the vet and said that we would take him.

When we picked him up a few days later he was already a different dog. He was still scrawny, with a dull, matted coat, but he seemed alert, if not exactly a bundle of energy. The vet estimated that he was about a year old, a mixed breed, predominantly German shepherd with some husky for good measure. At first he seemed shy and unsure, but after a few minutes of head scratching, chin scratching, and tummy rubbing, he decided that we were okay, and the three of us went home.

We named him Cody. We were happy to discover that he seemed to be housebroken, although the continuing symptoms of parvovirus (that is, severe diarrhea) made things a little difficult at first. As days went by we settled into a routine of early-morning, evening, and late-night walks in a nearby park. We hired a neighbor to walk him when we were at work. Cody quickly gained weight, and his coat became shiny and full. Suddenly he was a handsome, healthy dog. As we showered him with attention, he grew confident and secure, a happy dog who loved and trusted us.

About a year after Cody moved in with us, we bought a house. When accused by our friends of buying it for Cody, we don't deny it. Cody loves his backyard; he chases birds and squirrels and protects us from the daily invasion of the mailman. He has such a zest for life. Every game that we play, every ride in the car, every walk in

the park is a joyous occasion for him, as new and exciting as Christmas morning for a small child. He cherishes his head scratches and tummy rubs and all the love and attention that we give him. He is supremely confident of his place at the center of the universe.

It would be impossible to overstate what Cody has meant to Elizabeth and me. He returns our love for him many times over in the joy and love that he brings to us. When he entered our lives, he made us a family instead of a couple. Now that we have two children, Cody is still a focal point in our lives. We feel extremely fortunate to have found him.

We both had dogs before, but never one like Cody. Looking back, I don't know what we were thinking when we decided to take him despite the many eminently sensible reasons against it. It must have been our lucky day—better than winning the lottery!

LILA AND PETE

—— *Mia Edsall, Realtor* ——

Three years ago our daughter, Anna, persuaded us that we should get another dog. Of course we went to the pound. I can't imagine buying a dog when there are so many who need homes. Lila, a German shepherd cross, was about a year old when I first saw her. She had been at the shelter for two and a half months, lucky to be still alive after that much time. At some big-city shelters dogs are held only twenty-four hours.

I noticed Lila right away because of her eyes—soft, warm, and intelligent. She was pretty timid; in fact, we almost didn't take her because she was so terrified of the leash and she panicked about getting into the car. I think she must have been thrown around a little during that first year. She's very sensitive, just runs and hides if anyone yells at her.

At home she seemed insecure and anxious. She panted and whined, always wanting to be in your lap or under your feet. Then she started to settle down. She has always been good, no wandering, no chewing, no messes in the house, and, most important to me, she comes immediately when you call her. My husband, Steve, has always been skeptical about dogs, but even he likes Lila. I was afraid she might chase the horses, but that first week she got too close to one who kicked her so hard that she bit off the end of her tongue. As you might imagine, she's been cautious around them ever since. She does sometimes try to herd the cat.

When our pug (also a pound dog) died recently, we decided to get another small dog. We liked the idea of a poodle or a poodle mix. After visits to various shelters we finally met Pete, a cute, brown, wiggly six-week-old puppy, a pit bull/border collie mix. (Some miniature poodle!) But Anna and I fell for him, and that was that. At first he was tiny, so we encouraged him to be a lapdog and get on the couch with us. Now, at eighteen months and forty pounds, he still jumps on the couch and tries to sit on my lap—what a surprise!

I adopted these dogs because they needed me. I feel a responsibility to help homeless animals. When I look at Lila and Pete I know that I have done something good and that makes me happy.

GUINNESS

—— *Singer Rankin, Founder, World Women Work* ——

One day someone who knew I loved Jack Russell terriers called me about a little dog at the animal shelter in Santa Fe. The next day thoughts of this creature were still reverberating in my head, and of course I had to go right down there. It was an incredible scene—here was this frantic little dog jumping as high as the cage he was in, his right leg in a bandage all the way from his foot to his shoulder. He was to be put down that afternoon. I looked into his eyes; he was completely distraught. I just opened the cage door, picked him up, and said, "I will take him."

It turned out that he had been found on a country road about forty-five minutes from here. He had been run over and abandoned. His leg was so badly injured that it required amputation. By now his name was Guinness, and I took him directly to my vet, who agreed about the necessity for amputation. When a third vet concurred, Guinness had his leg amputated. As you might imagine, losing his leg was a very, very traumatic experience. I didn't really understand until later just how traumatic it must have been for him.

Not long afterward there was another major mishap. I was walking Guinness one night at dusk with the other dogs, Twigga, another Jack Russell, and Sam, my golden retriever. Guinness was on a leash because he was still recuperating, but when the other dogs took off, he pulled it right out of my hand and disappeared into the shadows. I went racing after them. Eventually

Twigga and Sam returned, but no Guinness. I finally found him in the hay shed covered with sand and gravel. I brought him inside and put him in my bathtub to clean him off. To my horror I discovered a huge puncture in his chest. We went off to the emergency vet who found that the dog's chest cavity had been pierced in many places, probably by a coyote. He almost died that time.

Just think about everything that he had been through—being lost or abandoned, then hit by a car and left there alone and suffering, his frantic time in the cage at the shelter, and now being mauled and nearly killed by a coyote. He has been unbelievable, but it took a whole year for him to become what I would call a real little Jack Russell. All of a sudden the playfulness began to come back, with all the energy and intelligence that is characteristic of these dogs. He began to tear around with Sam. They play by the hour, and Guinness is a real ball of fire; you would never know he has only three legs. He jumps just as high and runs just as fast as any four-legged dog.

From the day that I carried Guinness out of the shelter he has never left my side. He has slept on my bed every night since he first came here. He has completely taken over to such an extent that the other dogs have paled a little in comparison, but of course we don't tell them that. I have decided that from now on I'm going to take only three-legged dogs. It's my mission.

SPEC

—— Louise Crespi Benners, Competitive shotgun shooter ——

Spec is a piebald dachshund. With those spots he looks a little like a miniature pointer with very short legs. I call him my small quail dog for small Texas quail.

Spec started life as a stud dog in a puppy mill, not as much fun as you might think. Eventually the puppy mill was raided and all the dogs impounded. Spec, malnourished and infected with brucellosis, went to an organization that tries to save unfortunate animals like him. He was especially lucky then to meet up with Betty Taylor, who runs the car service I sometimes use. Betty rescues dogs frequently; she took Spec to try to find a home for him. As it happened, my old Westie, Taz, died while I was away on a trip, and when Betty met me at the airport, there was Spec in the backseat of the Lincoln. Betty said, "Why don't you try this one and see how you get along?"

Well, Spec was just so sweet I didn't even hesitate. After Taz died I was expecting to buy another dog. I had no clue that there were great dogs like Spec looking for a home.

The dog goes everywhere with me now. My children say he's changed my life. I don't go to the movies anymore; I just come home and hug the dog. At first he was frantic if I went out to lunch or something and left him, but he's better now. There's no telling what happened to him before (his ear had been chewed somewhere along the way), but I'll tell you one thing—this little dog has gone from the outhouse to the penthouse!

Spec doesn't care where he is as long as I'm there, too. I imagine he's the only dachshund on the shooting circuit. He travels right under my seat on the airplane, and I only stay at hotels where he's welcome, too. All these grown men on the circuit, these big shooters with Labradors and other large hunting dogs, they just love him. He has stolen everyone's heart.

I've never had a dog quite like him. He loves me more than any dog I've ever owned. I guess when you rescue them it's something special. My children are right; the dog has changed my life. How could you be in a bad mood with this sweet thing waiting for you at home? Can you believe a little dog like this could actually change your whole life?

GINGER

—— Karen Chapman, Receptionist ——

Ginger, my beautiful red-and-white border collie, was found, with a cat and a guinea pig, abandoned in a mobile home. It was thought that the animals had been there for at least two weeks before they were rescued. During this time Ginger had given birth to seven puppies, and the cat had produced five kittens. The animals had no food and were presumably drinking from the toilet. It is fortunate that they were found because the owner didn't return until two months later.

The neighbors told me that Ginger, as a puppy, had been kept hidden because pets were not allowed on the property. For months she stayed alone in a small metal storage shed. Eventually she was put out on a chain and became pregnant when she was about ten months old. Then she and the other animals were abandoned in the trailer.

The first time I saw Ginger her pups were near weaning age and she was thin, run-down, and depressed. I had been looking for a border collie and didn't really want to raise a puppy, so Ginger seemed like the perfect find.

I live out in the country on 120 acres, with a huge horse pasture, a creek, and a pond—all bordering a wildlife preserve. Ginger was absolutely thrilled with her new home. Like any self-respecting border collie she needed a job, so she immediately set to work chasing the ducks and geese off the creek. Their fear of her didn't last long, however, and it soon became a game. Another responsibility she has taken on is scaring magpies away from the bird feeders. She doesn't bother the smaller birds, but with the magpies she has an ongoing friendly feud.

Ginger's all-time favorite game is pretending that she is a ferocious cow dog. If you stamp your feet she nips gently at them, making all kinds of loud and fearsome noises. She loves to travel, but never strays. On days when she doesn't go to work with me she stays home and takes care of everything, including the two cats.

Ginger loves other dogs, horses, cats, and people, especially babies and small children. She will actually crawl on her stomach, using every kind of nonaggressive body language she can muster, in order to make friends with them. People tell me that she's the happiest dog they have ever seen because she's always smiling.

I have had Ginger for four years now, and I doubt that she will ever get over her fear of being abandoned, for she is one step behind me wherever I go. I don't mind, though, because she is the sweetest and most lovable friend I could ever imagine.

LUCILLE

—— Mike Mills, Musician with REM ——

One day a friend came into my house saying that there was a wild-looking dog in the yard who seemed to have been hit by a car. I went outside and, sure enough, there was this horrible-looking animal, barely recognizable as a chow. She had something wrong with her leg, her face was scraped up, and it looked like she had a bad case of mange. We found out later that her fur was just filthy and matted. She wouldn't let anybody get near her, however, so I called Animal Control. As soon as they saw her, they said, "Oh, we've been after her downtown for weeks. She's been hanging out with some other wild dogs, scrounging food wherever they can." I don't know how she got out to my neighborhood and into my yard.

Anyway, the Animal Control guys got a noose on her. I didn't like doing it because the dog was so scared, but it was really the only way to catch her. Then I took her to my vet. He fixed her up and then he came out and asked if I wanted her spayed. When I said, "Yes, of course," he told me that he had a cancellation and could do it the next day. Well, he called me after the surgery and said, "Everything's fine. She's okay, but it certainly is lucky that we spayed her. When I went in to do the surgery, I found that she was bleeding internally from a whole lot of little cuts in her liver, damage from the accident. If you hadn't wanted to spay her, we would never have known about this, and she would have surely bled to death."

The X rays didn't show this trauma, but they did show a fractured hip from the accident and some shot from a shotgun lodged in her tail. I guess she had a pretty tough life. But it got better.

Her hip healed by itself, and once we cleaned her up and put her on some good food, she became absolutely gorgeous. I would say that she's almost completely chow though she doesn't have that pure squished-up chow face. She has a little more of a bear look—maybe there is some Akita mixed in. She has this gorgeous red fur with black tips on parts of it. It's like a big fur coat. It *is* a big fur coat.

Right after Lucille moved in I had to go away on tour, but Tony, my neighbor and good friend, took care of her for me. I was away for a month and after I got back it took another month before Lucille would let me touch her. Even though she was living in my house and I was feeding her, she wouldn't let me touch her for almost five weeks. She's still a little skittish about strangers, men especially. I imagine that's where the abuse came from. But Lucille loves Tony, and his pound hound, Bender, is her best friend. Tony and Bender look after her when I have to travel; otherwise I really couldn't have a dog. I certainly owe a great debt to Tony.

Lucille is still nervous about going through doorways—I think she's had a door or two closed on her. She's been with me now for about a year, and she has turned out to be incredibly loyal and very protective of me and the house.

I think she must have had an owner some-where in her distant past because she did have a clue about *sit* and *shake*, but she was in such bad shape by the time I found her I wasn't inter-ested in knowing who it was.

Lucille is my companion. She's the one who's waiting there when I come home. She's the missing ingredient that turned my house into a home. You can have a great house to live in, but mine feels a lot more like home now that Lucille's here.

Somewhere in her doggy brain I suspect she knows she's landed in a good place. I think she's grateful, and that's why she's so good to me.

PETER PANDEMONIUM AND FRIENDS

—— Aline Lapides, Art dealer ——

Peter Pandemonium and Sheba Christina came to me when a local convent school for Native Americans was being closed down. The nuns were moving to other posts, and the dogs could not go with them. A friend of mine saw the notice in the paper, "Save the dogs of Saint Katy's!" and called me. We went right down to the convent and met Sister Ann Doyle and the two dogs, Peter and Sheba Christina. Sister Ann was very relieved to find a home for the dogs and better still a home where they could be together. She still comes to visit them from time to time.

Tara came from the shelter fourteen years ago. She's a happy, uncomplicated dog. She has always liked everyone and everything.

Emily, the little brown one, came from the shelter, too. She was pregnant when she was brought in, and no one loved her, though we do now.

Jessica Lee is the tiny lovely one. My manicurist found her on the highway. Her husband wouldn't let her keep the dog so she passed her on to me. At first my husband said, "It's that dog or me," but Jessie won him over. Now he's crazy about her. She does have a little attitude but I think that toughness saved her. When she was found she was so emaciated she had to be fed intravenously. She's a survivor.

I have four rescued horses as well. When they were saved, one of them was described as the thinnest horse anyone had ever seen still standing.

Some people think that taking care of all these dogs must be a lot of work, but it's not really work. It's just a matter of love and care. I have always loved animals. I don't care if they're old or sick or ugly. Over the years we have had quite a few. I really don't do it on purpose. Somehow they seem to find me.

GINNY

—— Philip Gonzalez, Retired steam fitter, animal rescue worker ——

About ten years ago at work I was involved in a bad industrial accident. I lost the use of my right arm, my knee was damaged, and I had some serious head injuries. I couldn't work. I stayed indoors because I didn't want to see anyone. It seemed like there was no reason to live. One day Sheilah, my neighbor and just about my last remaining friend, said to me, "We are going to the shelter to get you a dog so you will at least go outside to walk."

I thought if I had to get a dog I would get a big one, maybe a rottweiler, a Doberman, or a pit bull, something that could protect me. At the shelter the guy showed me the dogs he had there, but I didn't really like the big ones. Some of them were growling at me. Then the guy said he had a Doberman in back, a female with pups. I knew I didn't want a female, but I went to look at her anyway. While I was there the dog in the next cage got up, walked over, and started licking my hand. The guy said, "That's amazing. That dog has been here almost three weeks and it hasn't moved from that corner there. You are the first person it has come up to."

I said, "Yeah, you probably tell that to everybody."

Now, Ginny didn't have too much hair on her then so she looked a little like a baby German shepherd. I said, "I'll take him. He's a German shepherd, right?"

Then the guy told me that it was a female, a Siberian husky/schnauzer mix. She had been found with her three pups shut up in a closet in an abandoned apartment. I said, "Forget about it. I don't want a female."

But the guy said, "Listen, this dog really likes you." And Sheilah said, "Look, just take the dog for a walk and see how you like her." So to keep them quiet I took the dog out for a walk. Now, I was walking in front because I really didn't want anything to do with this dog. We had gone about a quarter of a block when she stopped and sat down. I turned around to tug on the leash. The dog was looking up at me, and she was smiling. I don't know what came over me but I looked in her eyes and I told her, "You are my dog and I'm taking you home."

From then on, Ginny stuck to me like glue.

About three days later, around 4 A.M., Ginny and I were walking by a vacant lot when a cat appeared. Ginny bolted toward the cat. She pulled the leash out of my hand just as the cat started toward her. I couldn't run because of my injured knee. I thought I was going to see a bloodbath, but when Ginny got up to the cat they started walking around each other. Then Ginny began kissing the cat, cleaning the cat. I thought, *This can't be happening. I must be imagining it because of the bumps on my head from the accident.*

The cat followed us home and Ginny whimpered and whined until I went in and got a can of dog food to feed the cat. That day I bought ten cans of cat food and a ten-pound bag of dry food. The next morning at 4 o'clock there were eight cats waiting for us. So then I got a case of cat food, twenty-four cans, and a twenty-pound bag of dry food. The next morning there were forty cats. They were weaving all around Ginny and she was licking them and cleaning them. They were skittish of me but not of Ginny. She was in all her glory cleaning cats.

So that's when I started feeding the cats.

A month later I said, "Ginny, since you're so much into cats I think I'll get you a cat for yourself. We won't take one of these feral cats. We'll

go to the shelter and get a cat who might be put down." At the shelter Ginny headed straight for the cat room and went around all the cages. She cried and whined in front of one cage; she wanted this kitten. I named the kitten Madame, and three days later I found out why Ginny had wanted her. Madame was completely deaf.

Three weeks later I said, "Okay, Ginny, now I'll get you a cat who can hear." This time she picked an injured cat, a cat with one good eye and one eye that was totally messed up. That was Revlon.

Then when Ginny was at the vet for her booster shots she spotted a kitten in a cage with a rope around its neck. The kitten was wild, hiss-ing at everyone, going ballistic, and Ginny was going crazy for this wild cat. The vet said, "I would advise against taking this cat. It's a wild feral cat and it will bite and scratch you. Besides, the cat has no rear paws." Well, that was Betty Boop. She hid out in her cage for three months until one morning I found her sleeping next to me on the bed. Now she's the sweetest cat going. She gets around all right. She hops.

One day Ginny ran into a vacant building and came out carrying a squirming kitten that couldn't move right. The vet said she had a con-dition like cerebral palsy in humans and the best thing would be to put her down. But how could I have this cat put down and have Ginny look at me and say, *What? You took my cat and had it put down?*

We still have the cat. She gets around okay, even uses the litter box. Instead of walking she rolls. I call her Topsy.

Ginny kept on finding more cats. One day it was a litter of kittens someone had dropped into a pipe; another time, a cat some people were kicking around like a football. I figure Ginny has rescued somewhere in the neighborhood of nine hundred cats over the years. They never scratch Ginny; they rub up against her and let her lick them. If I get too close, they try to do me in. One night Ginny was cleaning these kittens. The mother was right there watching and the kittens were all over Ginny. I figured, no problem. But when I tried to touch one the mother cat jumped on me and scratched me so bad that when we were going home my neighbors thought I had been shot. There was that much blood.

I find people to adopt a lot of the rescued cats, and we have quite a few at home. It's a small apartment, a sanctuary geared to animals. I got rid of most of my furniture; I have a small corner with my bed, and even there I usually wake up with one or two cats sleeping on me.

When I can, I try to catch cats, take them to the vet for shots and neutering, and then if I can't find homes for them, I release them where I found them. At least they're not producing more cats. People don't realize how cats can multiply.* Sometimes they tell me that every cat should have a chance to have kittens. Who do they think is going to feed those kittens?

After I wrote the book, *The Dog Who Rescues Cats,* Ginny was on the television show *America's Greatest Pets.* They flew us first class to California. Out there and on our book-signing tours we stayed in penthouse apartments, rode in stretch limos, and ate filet mignon. At least Ginny ate the filet mignon; I'm a vegetarian. The Westchester Cat Club gave Ginny its Cat of the Year award; she's the only dog who has ever won it, and the news went all over the world by radio, TV, Associated Press, and UPI. We got letters from Bosnia, England, Australia, you name it. Ginny has fans all over.

When I had my accident, the doctors wanted to amputate my arm, but I wouldn't let them. They did microsurgery to implant a stainless-steel rod and reattach some of the nerves, but they told me it would probably never move again. I was permanently disabled. I felt useless and depressed. But that was all before Ginny. Ginny to me is like an angel who gave me a life. I'm an animal rescue worker, self-employed and unpaid to be sure, but I'm happy doing this. Eventually my arm did move again, and I'm sure that being with Ginny made the difference.

The way I see it, I was Ginny's first rescue.

---

*The mathematics of feline reproduction: According to the Humane Society of the United States, one female cat and her offspring, assuming two litters per year and a survival rate of 2.8 kittens per litter, will produce 420,000 cats over a period of seven years.

SOPHIE, DURSTON, AND MURPHY

—— Sally Wagner, Retired owner-manager of a reservation trading post ——

All my dogs have been adopted. I found Durston, the older brown dog, at the shelter. I named him for my cousin.

Murphy, the whirling dervish, is only a year old. Like Durston, he came from the local shelter. I don't know much about his past, but I do know that he is terrified of flyswatters. I named him for a friend who has named several dogs after me. One day I noticed Murphy playing with something out in the side yard. He came over and dropped an old Navajo ring at my feet.

You might say that, at least that day, he sang for his supper. This dog is a study in perpetual motion. He torments poor Durston until I decide that Durston has had enough. Then I put Murphy out. Minutes later Durston, who is clever about these things, opens the door and lets Murphy back in.

Sophie, the big white dog who must be at least eighteen years old, used to belong to a friend of mine. Gradually I adopted her. I'm not quite sure how it happened.

MAJOR DEEGAN AND VIRGIL

—— *Kitty Hawks, Interior designer* ——

Rescued dogs have always been a big part of my life—Murphy and Earl the Pearl in California; then Lily, the world's only sedentary border collie; and more recently Major Deegan, Tyler, and Virgil. Deegan is the long, low, handsome black one. He had a rough start in life. I don't know anything about his history, but when he first arrived lots of things made him nervous. Coming back from a weekend in the country, he would start to pant and shake. He settled down gradually, but only became really comfortable several years later when I adopted four-month-old Tyler, a Samoyed/collie mixed breed. Tyler was smart and playful with a great sense of humor; he had never known anything but a good time.

When Tyler arrived, Deegan was a little jealous for a few days. But he had always loved other dogs and in spite of himself he began to enjoy the puppy. They played wildly, Deegan sometimes rolling along like a bowling ball. Deegan, seeing that Tyler wasn't afraid of anything, seemed to lose his own fearfulness. It was interesting to see how the younger dog made the older one more grounded.

Then Tyler died tragically and much too young. Deegan and I were both bereft. I was reluctant to take a chance on falling in love again, but after some months went by it didn't seem fair to Deegan, who was quite lonely and sad.

And so Virgil came into our lives. Apparently he was a stray who followed someone home. That someone gave him to someone else, who then decided that she couldn't keep him, either. He ended up at the Humane Society, where I first saw him. He seemed like such a sweetheart; I thought I would give it a whirl. It seems to be working out. Deegan has always been the alpha dog—in the nicest possible way. Virgil is learning manners, and he definitely is a sweetheart.

In the meantime, my husband, Larry Lederman, is a man who never had a dog in his life, and besides that he is very allergic to dogs. Nonetheless he has embraced them in every sense of the word. He walks them morning and night, refers to Deegan as his soul mate, and says he can't imagine life without them. I certainly can't imagine my life without them. I walk to the office every day because they go, too. Not only good exercise machines, they provide such a great outlet for affection. With them I can act extravagantly foolish the way you can with little children. My dogs are like heartworms; they have just burrowed right into my heart.

DUNCAN

—— Jody Cadenhead, Freelance copywriter ——

Seven years ago I lost two dogs very unexpectedly. One was a whippet, the other a whippet/greyhound mix. I was stunned; it was hard to absorb that kind of loss, never mind trying to get over it. A few months later I realized that I couldn't stand to be without a dog so I called a whippet rescue group in San Diego. They had two dogs, Duncan and Hanson, dogs who had lived together most of their lives and needed a home where they could stay together. At the time I had a huge yard and a roommate who was insane for dogs so I took them both.

Hanson died a few years ago, and even though the two dogs had been very close Duncan did not seem too traumatized. I think he always wanted to have me to himself anyway.

Duncan is fifteen now and very healthy although he has had a few little strokes. He's not quite as steady on his feet as he used to be but he still loves to walk; we go out every day. When we moved from southern California to the mountains of Idaho he adapted pretty easily. He wears a fleece coat and follows right along even when I snowshoe. Duncan is a good influence on me, especially now when I'm pregnant and feeling more and more like a couch potato. Our daily walk is definitely not optional. In fact we never miss a day.

Duncan is quite vocal—you might say outspoken—and not a bit shy about letting me know what his needs are. He likes to be covered with a blanket so he stands beside his bed and barks until I come over and pick up the blanket. Then he settles himself comfortably, turns around two or three times slowly, and finally lies down. Then I'm supposed to put the blanket over him. You can see that he has me well trained. He pretty much runs my life.

ANGEL

—— *Jeff Wynne, Filmmaker* ——

I had produced and directed a short film featuring an actor named Polly. When I stopped at Polly's house to drop off a DVD of the film, a little brown dog ran up to me and started jumping around my feet. She looked as if she might be part corgi and part Chihuahua with a little basenji around the tail. Polly told me that the dog had been picked up on the street in East LA by a homeless woman who lived in her car with a bunch of stray dogs, sometimes as many as fifteen. I guess it was quite a scene. Polly was trying to find a home for the dog, and suddenly I was a likely target. I said, "Give me a day or two to think this over, and I'll get back to you."

At first I thought my brother might take the dog, but then I decided she was perfect for me. When I went back to get her, Polly said, "It's really such a miracle that you happened to come by when the dog was here at my house. She was about to go to another foster home." And it was a total coincidence that I stopped by that day; it could have been anytime that week. With Polly's miracle in mind, I decided that *Angel* would be a good name for my new dog. Polly told me later that her kids had called the dog Angel while she was at their house—another coincidence.

Adopting Angel was pretty much an instinctive decision for me. She seemed to have a good disposition, she needed a home, and I liked her. Before, when I had thought about having a dog, I always felt that a dog would find me. And I guess this one did.

She's only been with me a short time so she's been going through some separation stuff. When I get out of the car, she starts clawing at the window even if I'm only going around to open the other door for her. If we go to a friend's apartment, after a few minutes she starts crawling into my lap, nervous that I might leave her there. I work at home so I've been able to spend a lot of time with her. If I'm busy on the computer, she curls up on the couch and lies around until it's time to go out again. She's very calm around the apartment; she is certainly smart enough to realize that it's a heck of a lot better here than where she was before. She's getting more relaxed about the times when I have to go out and leave her. She usually crawls into my bed or her bed and goes to sleep. I think she's starting to believe that she's not going to be abandoned.

At first Angel hid biscuits all around the apartment. Now she seems to know that the food supply is going to be there for her; that she can count on having enough to eat.

I've been trying to socialize her around other dogs, and she is a little more mellow, or at least better than she was. She can still be quite feisty. When she was living in that car, I'm sure she had to be seriously territorial to avoid being squashed.

This little dog is fitting herself right into my life. I think that it's part of a dog's nature to want human companionship. That's what Angel wants, and I'm happy to be her companion.

DJANGO

—— *Liz Teal, Dog trainer* ——

David and I had been looking for a dog for quite some time, but on that day thirteen years ago when we first met Django we were not exactly looking for a dog. We were looking for pants. As we walked past the ASPCA adoption van we saw a friend, Paul, holding a little puppy in his arms. As we said, "Hi," the puppy jumped from Paul's arms and I caught him. My husband looked at me and said, "It's him, isn't it?" And that was that.

Some kids in the Bronx had found Django in a trash can. They rescued the puppy and turned him over to the ASPCA. By the time Django was two years old he and I were involved in the ASPCA Visiting Pet program and the Delta Society Pet Partners. Both programs use evaluation procedures to assure that visiting animals are suitable for the work and that they will enjoy it. At one time or another Django tested almost every variation of the evaluation procedures.

Over the next seven years we worked with autistic children, developmentally disabled and/or mentally challenged children, cancer support groups, and children who were dying of AIDS. Django was very good at his job, and on more than one occasion he taught me valuable lessons. One day we were visiting a group of mentally challenged people, helping the teacher demonstrate grooming skills. Everyone took turns brushing Django. At the end of the session I said, "Django, let's go!" To my embarrassment, he refused to move. Then he pulled me to the back of the classroom and sat down in front of a kid with a very sad face, a face that broke into a huge grin when he saw that Django at least had not forgotten him. If everyone was supposed to get a turn, everyone got a turn. With a little egg on my face I learned to ask him if we were done, to trust his judgment.

When we started visiting AIDS patients, Django sometimes would go into a room and sit beside a person very quietly. The dog's whole affect changed. Often he would put his head on a knee if the patient was in a wheelchair or just rest it on the bed near a hand. Everything would get very still. The patient never spoke to me; occasionally a murmur to the dog. If I asked Django to leave, he wouldn't; he would just sit there. At first I thought this might be a sign of stress. Animals will sometimes become "deaf" when they are stressed and can't cope. But in these cases the dog seemed to grow roots. There was no way I could urge him away. Eventually, when he felt that it was time, he would get up and walk out the door, no stopping to say good-bye with a wave of the paw— he was saying it with a wave of his heart. These patients all died shortly after we left. I learned a new way of listening to my dog, a way that changed my life forever.

Django retired when he was about nine and started a second career as dog for all the neighborhood kids. This dog, rescued by kids, has spent most of his life returning the favor.

Now thirteen, he has had a stroke and liver complications, but he is still bright-eyed for his kids in the park. He walks very, very slowly from one group to another, checking up on everyone. At a post-September 11 candlelight vigil near our house I looked down to see Django sleeping nearby with a whole group of toddlers asleep on and around him. It was his gift to this crisis.

Django's own time to say good-bye is coming soon. As in so many lessons he has taught me, I

know that he will leave when his job is done, and I know that I will have his lessons with me for the rest of my life—lessons of justice, compassion, acceptance, and patience. He taught me the importance of listening, not just with my head, but with my heart.

The Delta Society Pet Partners program trains volunteers and screens their pets to work as therapy animal teams in health-related programs in health care and educational settings. For information, see www.deltasociety.org.

ROCKETT

—— Susan Garrison, Writer ——

About six years ago I had an iguana, and while I was away on a trip the house-sitter let the poor thing starve to death. When I came home and discovered this disaster, I went down to Animal Control to report it. While I was there a humane officer brought in a tiny puppy about six weeks old, a fluffball with blue eyes. The police had arrested a drunk with a puppy, and temporarily confiscated the puppy, which had to be held at Animal Control for ten days. I went down there every day to visit him and stick my fingers in the cage to pet him. When the waiting period was over I went to adopt him, only to be told that I didn't want this puppy because it was deaf. "Well," I said, "it's too late. He may be deaf but he's mine."

The dog certainly was deaf, and he has allergies. He doesn't see very well, either. He was born with subluxated pupils so he sees lights in a strange way. He hates anything flashing—cameras, Christmas tree lights, you name it. When I first had him, he would go berserk at the sight of a crutch or a cane. I think his first owner must have teased and tormented him.

I had a whole list of potential names for him, but when he was little he had a habit of shooting off to run as fast as he could. I call it his crazy-dog run, and because of it I named him Rockett.

I'm so neurotic about this dog that I brush his teeth regularly and one day I found a lesion on his gum. It turned out that he had a very virulent form of cancer. He was on chemotherapy for three years, and during that time I was diagnosed with breast cancer. Actually, we were both on chemo at the same time. At one point we were even taking the same medication. Rockett is always protective, but when I was sick, he was especially vigilant. He set up a perimeter around me and then started barking if anyone came too close. I had had a hysterectomy the year before the breast cancer, and Rockett guarded me day and night while I was recovering. He never once jumped up on me. He was so comforting.

As sweet as he is, Rockett will bite, but he mostly only bites members of the family, and then only if he thinks that he is being threatened or that I am being threatened. He doesn't like people on the street who seem to be unstable for any reason, and I'm not allowed to go near them. He'll bark and carry on and pull on the leash.

Rockett loves babies, and he's wild about my friend Billy. The dog goes crazy whenever he sees Billy and forgets all about me—you see, I'm just Mom. But at the same time I know that Rockett loves me, and I love him more than anything. I've given up friends and anything else that gets in his way.

SAM

—— Ann McLaughlin Korologos, Former U.S. Secretary of Labor ——

For thirteen years I had a basset hound, until he finally died of cancer. I waited a year, but then I thought it was silly to try to replace the dog with another basset. How can you ever replace a dog? So I went to the District of Columbia Animal Shelter, which is operated by the Washington Humane Society with the SPCA. I went there twice and the second time, there was Sam. He looked pretty much the way he does in the picture, but back then he weighed eight pounds instead of the nineteen pounds that was his normal weight. He had no hair at all except on his face and his back. The rest of him looked like a plucked chicken with these skinny little legs. The people at the shelter knew nothing about his past, just that there had been an anonymous call from a pay phone telling them to come and pick him up. They thought he was probably a mixed terrier, about nine months old.

When I met him, he jumped right into my lap. He was ready to go. He was much smaller than anything I had thought of bringing home, but when I looked at his face he was so bright. It wasn't so much that he was a cuddly dog; he was just so smart. I said to myself, *This is it— I've got to bring him home.*

Well, at this shelter you have to go through a lengthy adoption process, which is a good thing. Someone came to my house, looked at the yard, and interviewed me and the woman who takes care of the house. Finally we were approved, and Sam came home with me. At first I thought he could sleep on a pillow in the kitchen; that didn't last very long. He was so

good he moved right into the bedroom and for the next sixteen years that was where he slept. He certainly landed on Easy Street, and he got better and brighter every day. When I first met him, he needed me, and I just gave him a different kind of chance—it's a little like sending a kid to college. From then on Sam went through thick and thin with me. He was there for me and with me; he was that loyal and that strong. And he brought so much happiness to so many other people as well.

He flew everywhere with me, perfectly quiet in his little bag, so he had friends all over the place. People still ask about him.

When Sam was almost seventeen, we discovered that he had a nonmalignant tumor in his neck that made it hard for him to breathe. Surgery was out of the question; the tumor was too large, and Sam was too old.

Sam was with me when Tom and I got married, and for our first Christmas with the new family. Then I began to realize that he was really not himself. He would stand around and stare and look at the walls, much the way my grandfather had. It was that old-age kind of thing, just getting ready. My vet said to me, "You know, most people wait too long, and I think this dog seems depressed." I realized that she was right.

I used to say to him, "Sam, you've got to stay with me. It's just you and me." And he did stay with me—for over sixteen years. At the end Tom said, "Sam has done his job. He took care of you and now he has brought you to me. He's ready."

That dog was so special even at the end.

When I took him to the vet I was crying so hard I couldn't even tell them my name. I was holding Sam, and then he started to cough. My friend Jane said, "I think Sam is trying to tell you that he's ready." It was peaceful but I hadn't realized it would go so fast, that he would go so fast. You just had to let go.

Sam turned out to be everything I had hoped for when I first saw him. He certainly was good to me, loyal and very attached. Dogs who come up from hard knocks are special. It's both happy and sad that there will never be another Sam.

CASPER

—— Renny Reynolds, Designer ——

Over the years my partner, Jack Staub, and I have adopted all kinds of animals—five dogs, lots of cats, numerous birds, a few rabbits, and even a horse. We found Casper at the Bucks County SPCA. He was about a year old with a great look—part Lab, part Irish wolfhound. He was gazing out of the cage at us in a way that made it hard to walk on by. The former owners said that he needed more space, and he certainly did like to run. In his younger days (he's thirteen now) he was known as "The Bullet."

Casper is a good dog. He minds perfectly. The minute you whistle he's at your side. When I'm working in the garden he goes off exploring but periodically returns to check on me and to have a love moment. He is the most affectionate dog, really too big for a lapdog but he doesn't think so. He always goes with me to the office, where he likes to sleep under my desk. I have to put my feet on him or under him. This is fine except when we've just come back from the farm and he smells of pond muck. But clean or dirty, Casper is the best and most adoring dog.

ANNIKA, CHARLIE, MAGGIE, AND PIE

—— *Anita Wollmar, Retired executive* ——

The man from the electric company brings me dogs from time to time, and it was he who brought Maggie. She was a wild little French bulldog whose owner had ignored her as much as possible and hit her whenever she became too annoying. Her high energy makes her a handful, but with exercise and some new manners she is better now.

I found Charlie loose in the street dragging a twenty-foot chain, which was padlocked to her collar. She was very timid, so I had to chase her. I only managed to catch her when the chain got caught under a car. She is a chow mix with the temperament of a golden retriever.

I was at the shelter when Annika was brought in after being hit by a car. She's part Chihuahua, part God-only-knows-what. At first we thought her back was broken, but the vet discovered a broken pelvis and a fractured femur. Everything healed, but it was six months before she could walk properly. Even today she screams at the slightest injury, real or imagined.

When I first saw Pie wandering on the street, I thought that she was Sweetie, my friend's dog, until I learned that Sweetie was safe at home. Her double, Pie, was in my kitchen. I took Pie back to the neighborhood where I had found her and rang doorbells until I found a woman who said, "That dog has been living under a bush down the road. I can't imagine what she eats." Pie got along with all the other dogs, the temporary ones as well as the permanent residents, but she really loved my whippet. When he was eventually killed by a hit-and-run driver, she lay on his grave for three days. She whimpered and cried. For two months she wouldn't go for walks or do anything with the others. Then I brought Charlie home. Pie liked her instantly. That very day she decided to get up and take a walk with us. Then, of course, I had to keep Charlie. That was eight years ago.

These four dogs all have pretty good manners. When I bring home other dogs, and I always do, I need my dogs to be well behaved. I do try to find homes for all the dogs I pick up. I think that I really would like to have two dogs, but when you come back next summer, I will probably have five. I try not to, but . . .

C. J.

—— *Jorge Melara, Purchasing agent* ——

We went to the SPCA because my room-mate had been harping and harping about wanting a dog. He thought a dog would be good for picking up girls and hanging out. He didn't focus at all on what the dog might need. I didn't know much then, but I did know that a dog was a responsibility, a responsibility I was not prepared for.

I finally agreed to go to the shelter, but just to look, and mainly to make my roommate stop whining. We walked around the cages and saw all those desperate eyes telling their stories. It felt like they were saying, *They didn't feed me, it was so hot tied to that tree, I was left alone such a long time . . .* It hurt my heart to see them.

I spotted two dogs right away. One was a spotted spaniel mix, the other an American Staffordshire terrier mixed with Rhodesian ridgeback. We learned that a Staffordshire terrier is a type of pit bull. Whoa, a pit bull! So we took the spaniel mix into the meeting room, but he showed absolutely no interest in us. Then we tried the pit bull/ridgeback. His name was C.J. C.J. ran around madly jumping all over us. He licked and licked, then licked some more. He knew that this was his chance to get out of the kennel and away from his past. There were little spots on his head where the hair was missing. C.J.'s previous owners had burned him with cig-arettes; there were traces of gunpowder in his blood. I guess they were trying to make him a fighter, and when he wasn't, they threw him out.

Anyway, C.J. had decided; he chose us. He and my roommate convinced me that we should take him home. We learned later that C.J.'s days were numbered; if he hadn't found a home soon, they were going to have to destroy him. We had rescued an innocent life from death row.

C.J. was about eighteen months old when we adopted him. He had little or no training, and his accidents and puppy destructiveness were too much for my roommate. The honeymoon period wore off pretty quick, and I ended up caring for him most of the time. I became his dad; we were very close. I bought dog-training books to learn how to communicate with the dog, and slowly but surely he learned some basic obedience. The first and probably the most difficult thing was trying to figure out how to get his attention, how to get him to lis-ten to me. And while I was teaching him man-ners he was teaching me about unconditional love. All I did was to give C.J. the only thing I had—me—and that was all he needed. He taught me about responsibility because I wanted to be there for him. Instead of hanging out until all hours I would rush home to take care of my dog. C.J. introduced me to a new kind of people, dog lovers. I guess you could say they are a whole other breed.

We went through some tough times, espe-cially concerning finances and relationships. But no matter how bad things got I made sure that C.J. got his Purina, even if it meant that I did-n't eat. I was only twenty, still trying to figure out who the hell I was supposed to be. Growing up I didn't get the kind of love a child needs. C.J. helped me understand this. His uncondi-tional love made me realize that everything was going to be okay because he was in my life. It didn't matter if I left him for five hours or five minutes; he would greet me just the same when I got home, his tail wagging in wild circles while he did his little dance of joy.

C.J. changed my life and he has affected the lives of many other people as well. Even those who are not dog lovers fall for him. Some of his fans have gone out and adopted dogs themselves,

some have volunteered their time for rescue work, and others have simply become more knowledgeable about dogs in general. I discovered that by owning a pit bull mix I needed to educate people about the breed. Believe me, there is a lot of misinformation out there. People who see how sweet and intelligent C.J. is sometimes don't believe me when I tell them that he is part pit bull.

It has taken about five years to undo one year of abuse. C.J. still gets a little nervous around a mop or a broom, though he is much, much more confident than he used to be. I work with him every day in the safety of our home, and that helps. He likes to learn tricks. This year, at the Great American Mutt Show in New York, he won the class for Most Creative Pet Trick, a kind of shell game with a biscuit hidden under one of three paper cups. He went on to win Best in Show. We were interviewed by all these newspapers, magazines, and TV news programs. We even went on *Good Morning America*.

C.J.'s first trick was shaking hands. For the shake I tried a way of teaching I had learned when I was working with autistic children. I would say the word *shake* and take his paw. He got it right away, just like a duck to water. The *speak* trick came one evening when I was doing this odd whistle. C.J. cocked his head and let out a *woof*, so I whistled, gave the command, and rewarded him with a cookie. I can usually get ten to fifteen minutes of focused time from him now. You have to build up to it. He knows that he can make the rewards come. I think a lot of it boils down to the way he wants to please. He sees how happy I am, and he says to me, "See, Dad, I did it! *Woo hoo!*"

For information on the Great American Mutt Show, visit www.tailsinneed.com/dogshow.

DEO

—— Basil Service, Title examiner, ski instructor ——

My mom found Deo. He was scrounging around garbage cans and Dumpsters. He was so wild that she couldn't catch him, but finally some neighbor kids caught him for her. He was unbelievably skinny; the vet said that he could have died. Mom kept him for a while. My brother called him D-O-G, which I shortened to D-O or Deo. When I moved to another part of the state, Deo went with me. Actually, my brother slipped him into my car as I was driving away. Anyway, he was mine then.

For a long time Deo seemed to think that he needed food caches in case the bad times returned. He would take stuff from the garbage or the kitchen counter and hide it around the house. Once, soon after he came to live with me, two trays of brownies disappeared from the top of the refrigerator. I found most of them under pillows or furniture and figured he had eaten the rest. Not a good idea since chocolate is poisonous for dogs. Later I put some wet ski clothes in the dryer, and soon the house smelled like brownies baking. And brownies were baking—in the dryer. House guests sometimes found stale bagels under the pillows on their beds. One time I set up a video camera in the kitchen and left some steak on the counter and some prime rib on top of the refrigerator. In less time than it takes to tell about it, Deo had gotten all that food down and eaten it—on the carpet in the living room, of course. He sleeps on the bed, too.

I do a lot of hiking, backpacking, and climbing in the mountains. At first I left Deo at home because I was afraid that he couldn't keep up. You know, he's not very big. Then one weekend I took him on a twenty-mile hike, figuring that I could put him in my pack when he got tired. But he never did get tired, he just kept on going, chasing squirrels and having a great time. After that he went everywhere with me. He has been with me on three twelve-thousand-foot peaks and many, many smaller peaks. It's only on the really technical climbs that I leave him in camp, and then I have to tie him with a chain because he chews right through rope to follow me. He even goes with me when I'm ski mountaineering. He stays right on top of the snow because he's so light.

He does enjoy hunting. Once he treed a black bear. I thought, *No one will believe this*, so I took pictures to prove it. He's gotten involved with porcupines only twice. Once he went after a coyote. The coyote turned and picked him up. Deo apparently objected, because the coyote dropped him pretty quick, and Deo ran off. After that he stayed a little closer to me for a while.

He still does take off from time to time. He was gone once for five hours. I finally decided to go get some stuff so that I could spend the night waiting for him, but he showed up on the trail out, at least three miles from the spot where he had disappeared.

Deo is a good dog. He's a tough dog *and* a lapdog.

CHEKA

—— Donna Shalala, President, The University of Miami ——

I first met Cheka at La Guardia Airport when he was ten weeks old. His new owner, Dr. Elizabeth Karlin, had asked me to bring him with me to Madison, Wisconsin. The plane was delayed for hours because of bad weather in Wisconsin, but Cheka worked the crowd happily until we boarded. Meanwhile I called Liz and suggested that she meet us in Milwaukee so that the puppy wouldn't have to take another plane after such a long day.

In Milwaukee he bounced out of his crate, trotted outside for a pee, greeted Liz, and then settled down on my lap for the ride to Madison—already a world class schmoozer and snuggler.

Over the next year and a half Liz and I frequently walked our dogs together. Cheka always had a stuffed animal in his mouth. He took it wherever he went. Then I left Madison and saw Cheka only occasionally, although Liz and I kept in touch.

When my dog died I decided not to get another until I had finished government service. Then one day I learned that Liz had been diagnosed with an inoperable brain tumor. I visited her often and was touched to see that Cheka insisted on spending most of his time at her bedside. Liz was very worried about what would happen to him. Her children, in graduate school and just starting their careers, couldn't take on the responsibility of a dog, particularly an older dog.

As I looked at Liz and her beloved pet I thought, *What better gift could I give my friend?* I nodded my head. "Send him to me," I said. Liz smiled—it was our last visit.

Shortly thereafter, Cheka arrived in Washington by plane. I went to meet him, and he emerged from the crate with a teddy bear in his mouth. I burst into tears—he looked so sad and scared. He was quite depressed for about four months. The dogs in our neighborhood park were gentle and friendly. They seemed to bring him out of his sadness.

Cheka definitely is a character—all personality. He works a crowd better than any Washington politician. His name means "laughter" in Swahili, and he really is the best medicine I know.

LIZA DOOLITTLE

—— Joanne McGarry, Executive secretary ——

Just before Halloween a few years ago, a scruffy little terrier mix, very pregnant, was picked up wandering the streets. The next day seven pups were born. Mother and babies were temporarily safe, but if they were not claimed during the stray period all would have to be euthanized. Fortunately, one of the San Francisco SPCA hearing-dog trainers was making the rounds at area shelters looking for recruits for the program. When the trainer stopped in front of the cage with the mom and babies, Mom took a much-needed break from nursing to come up front and introduce herself. The trainer tried a few preliminary sound tests and thought this might be a good hearing-dog candidate.

At four days old the puppies were too young to leave their mother, but the trainer was able to make arrangements to bring the whole family to the SPCA where they would be placed with a foster family until the pups were old enough for adoption. Then Mom would move upstairs to the Hearing Dog Program. I was working at the shelter and met the family when they arrived there. I couldn't help noticing the terrier mom with the doe-like eyes. I even said to the trainer, "That's my kind of dog."

After a medical check and a brief stay at the shelter, mother and pups moved in with a loving foster family. As weeks went by the puppies grew while Mom proved herself to be a sweet-natured, gentle animal, getting along well with the family, including the young children and the family dog.

Thanksgiving passed. Christmas grew near

and the puppies were ready for adoption. The seven little dwarfs had grown into seven roly-poly pups looking for loving homes, and in no time at all they found them. Making their debut in the holiday windows at the San Francisco Shopping Center, all seven found new friends who adopted them.

Meanwhile, terrier Mom moved into the Hearing Dog Training Center to start her new career. However, it seemed that her street days spent fending off dominant and unaltered male dogs had left her more than a little defensive—not a good trait for a service dog. She was not going to make it as a hearing dog.

The three-day Martin Luther King weekend was approaching. The shelter already had a full house of canines awaiting adoption so I, unsuspecting, offered to take the little dropout home for the holiday to give her a break from the kennels.

Love blossomed over the weekend as I quickly realized that Liza was not going back to the SPCA, at least not to be put up for adoption. As it happened, she returned there to work in the administrative offices, sitting under my desk and generally keeping an eye on everything and occasionally going out on a special project. She visits schools as part of a humane education program. In one year she met over seventeen hundred kids. I think she must have the Guinness record for Most Pawshakes.

A dog who once had nothing and no one, Liza's not looking back. In fact, she's looking adoringly into my face as I look back with a heart full of love.

SHERMAN

—— *David Brock, Writer* ——

I have a friend, an inveterate animal lover, who dropped by a shelter in Wilmington, Delaware, a couple of years back on a road trip to the beach. My phone rang in Washington on Saturday morning, reporting a remarkable discovery: A large, curly-haired black beast was available for adoption, and my friend thought we would be perfect for each other. Something in the eyes, apparently. I drove to Wilmington and fell in love.

Sherman, I called him. He had been picked up as a stray. Sherman was smart, sensitive, serious, well mannered at home, one of the gentlest beings on four legs I had ever known. But Sherman had a problem. Whenever he glimpsed another dog, he jumped out of his skin and screamed like a banshee. So for months, on the advice of two trainers and a doggy psychologist, who grimly pronounced Sherman improperly and permanently unsocialized, I tried to avoid other dogs. We ducked into alleys and hid behind cars. We ran on a tennis court instead of in the park. We tried all manner of restrictive leads. We played fetch in the foyer. Though it seemed impossible, the problem got worse.

Then one day I arrived to pick up Sherman from a new groomer. The old groomer had followed my copious instructions that Sherman be shielded from contact with other dogs, even to the point of scheduling other dogs to accommodate Sherman's comings and goings. But he soon closed up shop. Distracted that morning, or perhaps in denial, I dropped Sherman at the new groomer with no warning and sped off. When I returned, Sherman bounded out from a large pen, where he had been housed with a dozen dogs from the adjoining day-care center. My heart raced as I looked on in horror, then in disbelief. When I told the groomer of Sherman's troubled history, she looked up and said nonchalantly, "I usually ask first, but he seemed so nice, I just put him with the other dogs. He must have a leash problem." This possibility was news to me.

When I related the potential breakthrough to my boyfriend later that afternoon, he insisted on marching Sherman up to the neighborhood dog park three blocks away and letting him off his leash. The walk was difficult, as always. I hid behind a car as James and Sherman passed through the forbidden gates. Unbound, Sherman bounced with joy from dog to dog, then led them around in a little parade, the Pied Piper of dogs. An elderly Georgetown matron pronounced, "Sherman's a hit."

And I was left wondering if the problem was more my fear than Sherman's.

NAANEES

—— Rita Oliva, State police secretarial supervisor ——

Three years ago my neighbors' in-laws found a little dog abandoned in the basement of an apartment complex. They called me and I said, "Of course we'll take him." Over the years my husband and I had rescued many dogs, but I had never seen anything like this poor little thing. Every one of his toes had been broken; his nose and jaw had been broken, and his tail as well. He was about ten years old, a miniature dachshund, emaciated, just hair on a skeleton, and terrified. Within twenty minutes we were at the animal hospital. The vet told us that in addition to the injuries and starvation the dog had serious heart trouble and cataracts. I just looked at the doctor and said, "Please, won't you give him a chance?"

So they operated, putting a pin and wires in his jaw. He was in bad shape after the surgery; no one thought he would make it through the night. To everyone's amazement he was still alive the next morning, and from then on he seemed to get a little stronger every day. We named him Naanees—it's an Italian endearment.

I can't imagine how anyone could have hurt him, and if I ever find the person who did it . . . For months he was frightened of everything. He was hand-shy, even with us. For the first year he never barked at all. Now he feels secure, and when someone comes in he barks up a little storm. If it's a stranger he burrows under my arm to hide. Sometimes he cries in his sleep. His nose is still very crooked, and we have to feed him with a spoon, but we don't mind. We get back so much love in return. My husband dotes on him. He is retired so they stay home together.

When we found him, he needed us. Now we need him. Sixteen months ago our son, Adam, died suddenly of an aneurism at the age of twenty-one. The comfort Naanees has given us is beyond belief. He likes to go for a ride; he always goes with us to visit our son's grave. We have had many dogs and we have loved them all, but none compare to this little buttercup. Naanees has become our "baby"; we treat him as such, and he eats it right up. He had suffered so much before we found him that we have tried to make up for all the bad times and to give him nothing but good.

Naanees has his own charm. He looks at you with that little lip hanging, and you just want to cuddle him. Every month I buy him a new outfit and he gets all dressed up to go for a checkup. All the people at the animal hospital love him. He's a success story for them, too. Last time he wore his new biker outfit, black leather jacket with chains and a little cap, also with chains. The vet took one look at him and said, "Rita, he looks like he's going to a leather bar!"

I haven't a clue what I will do when his time comes. I hope God keeps him around another twenty years.

JASMINE

—— William Blair, Retired lawyer and diplomat ——

I have always loved dogs, and when Wendy, Jasmine's predecessor, died at the age of twelve, the house seemed very empty. I get my dogs from shelters, so I began making the rounds in search of a small dog. There seemed to be no small dogs at that time, but eventually I got a call from a shelter in Maryland. They said that they had a small dog, but one whom I probably wouldn't want. She had been abandoned on a highway. No one wanted her, and they were going have to put her away. "Oh, don't do that," I said. I got in the car and drove right over.

I found a small terrier mix in a large pen, all alone and shivering. She was obviously terrified; they had to drag her out to see me. There was no tail wag, no response. She had a large tumor on her back; she was dirty and covered with fleas and ticks. She looked so pathetic that I decided to take her and give her a try.

We went immediately to the vet's. In the car she was wild, racing back and forth and careen-ing from window to window. I left her at the vet's so that they could remove the tumor and clean her up. Five days and five hundred dollars later, the biopsy proved benign, and I brought her home.

I have had Jasmine now for a year and a half. She's sweet with the people she likes and espe-cially sweet with me. She likes to sit on my lap all the time when she's not preoccupied with bird and squirrel patrol. She has established a no-fly-zone around the house. She is also vigilant about squirrels, often spotting them from inside the house and racing off to chase them. My wife thinks that she's a bit frenetic, but she has a lot of spirit, which I like in a dog. She nibbles on you if you're not paying enough attention.

I have always had dogs, and they have been an important part of my life. My son used to work in an office, but he missed being outdoors and with dogs, so he decided to become a pro-fessional dog walker. I am probably to blame.

DUFFY

—— Gordon Peterson, TV news anchorman ——

This is a Christmas story. The National Cathedral here in Washington is a wonderful place, especially at Christmas when it is warm and welcoming. But a few Christmases ago, on Christmas Eve to be exact, the weather was foul, and a little dog, a stray—wet, miserable, hungry—was trying to get in without success. There was no room for him in that magnificent edifice on that Christmas Eve.

But a couple of friends of mine, Jack and Kitty Wainwright, were at Christmas Eve services. Afterward they came out, they saw the dog, they scooped him up, they took him home, they cleaned him up, they fed him. They determined he was a stray. Because they already had a dog, they asked me if I would take him.

I resisted at first, but one day when I walked into their living room, the dog jumped up into my arms and kissed me and hugged me. Jack said, "God sent you that dog—don't turn your back on him!" What could I do?

What I didn't know was that Duffy loves to sing. He sits right beside me on the piano bench so that I can accompany him. He would rather sing Christmas songs than anything. He likes classical music, too, especially chamber music. He likes World War II songs. He hates rock-and-roll and country-and-western. But of course, Duffy loves Christmas music best. He's a Christmas dog.

P. D.

—— Sue Blagden, Rancher ——

I suppose P.D.'s story starts when my friend, Mickey Reynolds, called to tell me about her Aunt Cora who, at the age of ninety, had recently lost both of her elderly Chihuahuas. She had taken them with her everywhere and, of course, she felt lost without them. I called Aunt Cora to commiserate and offered to look for a dog for her. "No, dear," she said sadly. "I'm much too old to have another dog. It wouldn't be right."

Two months later Aunt Cora was on the phone again. "Sue, I just can't do without a little dog. I've tried and I can't stand it. Do you think you could find me a dog who looks something like a Chihuahua, a housebroken dog who will sit on my lap?" I promised to try.

I put feelers out all over the place with various rescue friends, and several days later one of them called about a little dog at a shelter near here. The dog had been seen wandering beside the highway for three days before he was picked up. My friend described him as "vaguely Chihuahua-like, though larger with a little terrier thrown in." He seemed sweet.

We were having a blizzard that day so I couldn't make the two-hour trip to check him out, but the next day the traveling ballet teacher brought him over with her. When he came out of the crate at ballet class I thought he was the ugliest little dog I had ever seen. I guess he looked a tiny, tiny bit like a Chihuahua and he did like to sit on laps, but he most definitely was *NOT* housebroken. I kept him anyway.

I took him home and fastened the end of his leash to my belt so that I could keep track of him. He didn't seem to mind; in fact he wanted to follow me around most of the time anyway. We called him P.D. (short for Puppy Dog). I carried him inside my coat when I went out to feed the cows and kept him with me all the time. Within a couple of weeks he was completely reliable in the house. (I think neutering helped.) The bad news was that, at the other end of the leash, I had become very attached to this funny little dog.

But I had promised Aunt Cora, and so, a few days before Christmas, Mickey and her husband picked up P.D. to take him over to Portland. He looked pretty cute in his red collar with a big red bow. I reminded Mickey to tell Aunt Cora that I would love to take the dog back if, for any reason at all, he didn't work out; then they drove away. I sat down and cried.

A week later I got a card from Aunt Cora with a photograph of herself holding P.D. on her lap. On the back she had written, "The best Christmas ever!"

Aunt Cora loved that little dog and for the next six months the two were inseparable. Then one day Aunt Cora had a fatal stroke. Her son found her with P.D. in her arms.

They remembered that I had said I would love to have him back, and I've had him ever since. He fit himself right into our family with our three daughters, five dogs, five cats and Winston, the potbellied pig. I certainly didn't need a little dog or any kind of dog, but P.D. was irresistible.

Now he's very old and very smelly, and we love him.

ADOPTING A DOG

DO YOU *REALLY* WANT A DOG?
These are a few questions to consider:

1. What exactly are you looking for in a dog?
Are you looking for companionship; a partner for long walks, for strenuous hikes in the mountains, or sitting together on the sofa; company in the office; or all of the above; or none of the above? Would you like a dog to work with, perhaps in Animal Assisted Therapy or agility trials or search and rescue? How do you see a dog sharing your life?

2. How will a dog actually fit into your life?
Realistically, how much time do you have to devote to care, exercise, grooming, and training? Do you travel? What will you do about vacations? Dogs need companionship; they are social creatures, pack animals, not stuffed toys to cuddle with when you are in the mood and ignore the rest of the time. A dog who does not get enough attention will be an unhappy dog and probably a nuisance as well. If you work all day, leaving your dog at home alone, and have classes, meetings, and social events in the evenings, you might want to consider adopting a cat. Some cats are quite content to have the house to themselves during a major part of the day as long as they are fed well and given attention when they demand it. If you have a fairly sedentary lifestyle or if you are away for long hours, consider an older dog—not just an adult dog but actually an older dog. These mature sweeties have usually settled down and may demand less of your time.

3. Are you looking for a dog to be a companion and playmate for a dog you already have?
This can be tricky. Often a dog with "too much energy" is not getting enough attention from his human companion; adding another dog to the family can make the situation worse. Never bring two new dogs or puppies into your life at the same time. They will bond to one another, and you will be peripheral at best. If you do already have a dog and decide to get another, one of the opposite sex and of roughly equal size is usually the best choice.

4. Are you looking for a dog of a specific breed?
Try not to be seduced simply on the basis of looks. Consider temperament, activity, size, and especially what that particular breed is designed to do. Hunting dogs may retrieve anything that is not tied down, and they are apt to roam if unsupervised. Some herding dogs have such an intense desire to work that they need a job or at least an owner who is prepared to spend time training them and giving them an occupation, whether it be herding, agility trials, or something else. Otherwise these dogs will find jobs for themselves—and this may involve chasing cars.

Be aware that some breeds have a predisposition to medical problems such as hip dysplasia, deafness, seizures, or various forms of cancer.

Learn about different breeds and what you can expect from them. This knowledge can be useful in evaluating mixed-breed dogs as well as purebreds. Talk to dog owners, trainers, vets, and shelter personnel. Educate yourself. Read.

5. When to adopt?

This is highly variable and depends on your individual situation. The busy holidays are not a good time to bring a new pet into your home and into your life. Never give a friend a pet as a surprise; it often ends badly for the pet.

5. Can you afford a dog?

Try to anticipate, at least in a general way, the expense involved in providing good-quality dog food, boarding if you travel, training classes (don't economize here—it's the best possible investment), and of course medical costs. Even a young, healthy dog needs immunizations and may have an accident or injury.

HOW TO START A SEARCH FOR THE DOG OF YOUR DREAMS

Once you have evaluated your situation, have decided that you *do* want to look for a dog, and have a sense of what kind of dog you would like, what next?

1. Some **veterinarians** place homeless animals.
2. **Animal shelters**, sadly, are usually full of candidates for adoption. Check them out—large municipal shelters and both large and small private ones.
3. There may be **individuals** in your neighborhood who work in an informal way to place homeless animals.
4. Check the **Internet**. Try searching "pet adoption," "dog adoption," "animal shelters," and so forth.
5. If you are interested in a specific breed, contact the **American Kennel Club** for information on rescue groups for that breed. Remember, purebred dogs do turn up at shelters as well.

Tips for going "just to look" at a shelter, a veterinarian's, or a foster home:

1. Talk with the people caring for the animals.

Explain what you are looking for. Ask about the dog's history and temperament. If you sense that they don't have time for this or are trying to talk you into taking an animal simply because it needs a home ("If you don't adopt her, she'll be euthanized tomorrow"), go somewhere else. Responsible people in the business of placing animals understand the importance of making a good match. After all, they are the ones who see the sad results of decisions made on impulses like "What a cute puppy! Wouldn't it be fun to have one!"

2. Consider an adult dog.

A puppy can be a surprise package. An adult dog may give you a better sense of how he will turn out, though of course you must allow for temporary depression or overexcitement caused by stress.

3. Do not bring children, especially young ones, with you to help choose a dog.

It is a sure route to an impulse choice that you may regret later. Wait until you have a good idea of the dog you think is best for your family; then bring the children in to see how they and the dog interact.

4. Do not take a dog simply because you feel sorry for the poor thing.

With any luck the dog you adopt may be with you for ten or fifteen years, perhaps longer, and it is just as important for the dog's sake as it is for yours that the relationship be a happy and successful one.

5. Visit the dog several times before making a decision.

Take her for walks if possible; notice how she responds to other dogs and to people. If you feel at all unsure, go to other shelters and look at other dogs.

6. Bring family members and possibly other pets to meet a dog whom you are seriously considering.

This is an exception to #3 above; in this case you are bringing children to meet a specific dog, not presenting them with the option of any dog at the shelter. If you have cats or other pets, you will want a dog who doesn't chase or, worse still, kill them.

7. Take your time.

This is an important decision and a major commitment. Talk it over with people whom you respect, especially people who have had experience with dogs. Think about it. Sleep on it.

BRINGING YOUR NEW DOG HOME

Plan ahead

1. Make an appointment for a veterinary checkup for your new dog as soon as possible.

Plan to bring records of any known immunizations as well as a stool sample. You may also want to schedule an appointment with a groomer.

2. Shop for supplies:

A **dog crate** of an appropriate size with a washable bed will give your dog a den of his own, a place where he will be safe. If he is in a crate, he cannot chew electrical cords or leave puddles around the house. Do not leave the dog in the crate for long hours. Use common sense.

Dog food that the dog has been accustomed to will make the transition to a new home easier and stomach upsets less likely. If you decide to switch foods, do so gradually—substitute a little more of the new food each day. Discuss quality dog food with your vet and/or the staff at a good pet store.

Bowls for food and water.

Toys that are safe to chew are important for teething and for entertainment. Toys stuffed with your dog's kibble are great entertainment when he's in his crate.

A collar with a name tag (your address and phone number), a leash, and a long line.

3. Dogproof your home as much as possible.

Remove potentially dangerous objects as well as things that could be damaged. Designate an area where the dog can comfortably spend time with you. Do not give a new dog the run of the house.

4. Decide with your family or roommates what the rules are to be.

This way you can all help the dog learn from the very beginning. Consistency is extremely important.

The Big Day

You fill out the adoption forms, pay the fees, and take your new dog home with you. It is an exciting experience, the beginning of a new relationship.

1. Introduce family members and pets in a controlled way.

Keep the atmosphere calm and quiet. Never leave a new dog unsupervised with children or with other pets until you have a good sense of the dog's potential reaction, not to mention the reaction of the child or pet in residence. This will take weeks or longer, not days. Children must be supervised and trained to be gentle with animals, for their own sake as well as the animals'.

2. Use the crate.

This will help with house training and destructive behavior. Remember, prevention is often the best training. Feeding the dog in her crate and leaving her there with kibble-stuffed toys can make this den more appealing. Do not reward barking, scratching or whining by letting the dog out of the crate. Wait until she is quiet. Be sure that she goes out to relieve herself often enough so that you know she is not yelling, *Emergency!*

3. Spend as much time as you can with your dog, especially in the beginning.

Plan to bring the dog home over a weekend or, better still, during a vacation. During this time occasionally leave the dog alone in the crate for short periods so she can learn that your departure does not mean abandonment.

4. Be patient.

Remember that your dog has been through some stressful, perhaps even traumatic, experiences and will need time to settle down and to learn what you expect. Leave a leash or a long line on the dog in the house so that you can easily call him to you—don't forget treats when he reaches you! Keep a bag of something delicious in your pocket at all times.

Look for professional help right at the beginning. Sign up for classes. *Prevention* is the watchword: Set your dog up to succeed. Try to anticipate his actions in order to avoid letting him make mistakes. Orchestrate situations so that you can say "Good dog!" rather than "Bad dog!" Be prompt and generous with compliments and rewards for good behavior. Use a positive approach; your dog will learn quickly and easily.

5. Exercise is important.

Both you and the dog will feel better and probably behave better as well. Check with your vet on the appropriate level of exercise. You can overdo it, especially with puppies, older dogs, dogs with physical problems, or dogs who have been leading a sedentary life. Start out slowly, use common sense, and take your cues from the dog. Remember, most dogs are eager to please and will overtire without complaining.

6. Enroll the dog in an obedience class.

This involves an investment of time and money that will really pay off in the long run. It can make all the difference in helping a dog become a great companion.

Do some careful research before choosing a trainer. Ask friends who have had successful experiences with obedience classes. If possible, attend a class as an observer. You should be comfortable with the training methods and the way the trainer treats students, both human and canine. A trainer who kicks or hits a dog or suspends one by the collar is a trainer to avoid. A good trainer will understand the importance of tailoring all training to the individual. Methods that might be effective with a dominant, strong-minded dog would not be appropriate for a more submissive, timid dog. Sometimes secondhand dogs have had bad experiences with humans, making them fearful and insecure. Training based on positive reinforcement usually works best, and in my experience it's a lot more fun.

Your job is to learn how best to motivate your own dog. A trainer can be a valuable ally in your efforts to include your dog in your life. A well-behaved, socialized dog can visit friends with you, travel with you, share vacations, and perhaps even accompany you to work.

There are many good books on dog training. (See Recommended Reading.) They are most effective when used in conjunction with actual classes.

Work with your dog, include this dog in your life, and above all, enjoy your dog!

As an unknown writer points out, "He is your friend, your partner, your defender, your dog. You are his life, his love, his leader. He will be yours, faithful and true, to the last beat of his heart. You owe it to him to be worthy of such devotion."

ACTIVITIES TO SHARE

GENERAL
The American Kennel Club
260 Madison Avenue
New York, NY 10016
www.akc.org
(212) 696-8200
The AKC can provide information on clubs involved in many different activities, such as agility, obedience, herding, tracking, carting, and sled pulling.

The Great American Mutt Show
www.tailsinneed.com

The United Kennel Club
100 East Kilgore Road
Kalamazoo, MI 49002-5584
www.ukcdogs.com
The UKC can provide information on many different activities, including agility and obedience trials. Mixed-breed dogs who are neutered/spayed may participate.

AGILITY
United States Dog Agility Association
P.O. Box 850955
Richardson, TX 75085-0955
www.usdaa.com
(972) 487-2200
(972) 272-4404 fax

OBEDIENCE COMPETITION
The American Mixed Breed Obedience Registration
(also agility and other activities)
179 Niblick Road, #113
Paso Robles, CA 93446
www.amborusa.org
(805) 226-9275 telephone and fax

Association of Pet Dog Trainers
17000 Commerce Parkway—Suite C
Mount Laurel, NJ 08054
www.adpt.com

PET-ASSISTED THERAPY
The Delta Society
580 Naches Avenue Southwest, Suite 101
Renton, WA 98055-2297
www.deltasociety.org
(425) 226-7357
(425) 235-1076 fax

The Good Dog Foundation
607 6th Street
Brooklyn, NY 11215
www.thegooddogfoundation.org

Check the Internet for other activities such as dog camps, Frisbee, herding, lure coursing, and skijoring/sledding. Don't forget walking, hiking, swimming, backpacking, and camping—all activities that are fun to share with a dog.

RECOMMENDED READING

Animal Fair magazine, www.AnimalFair.com.

Bailey, Gwen. *Adopt the Perfect Dog: A Practical Guide to Choosing and Training an Adult Dog.* Reader's Digest, 2000.

Branigan, Cynthia A. *Adopting the Racing Greyhound.* New York: Howell Book House, 1993.

Donaldson, Jean. *The Culture Clash.* James and Kenneth Publishing, 1997.

Dunbar, Ian. *Before You Get Your Puppy.* James and Kenneth Publishing, 2001.

—— *After You Get Your Puppy.* James and Kenneth Publishing, 2001.

Gonzalez, Philip, and Leonore Fleischer. *The Dog Who Rescues Cats: The True Story of Ginny.* HarperPerennial, 1995.

—— *The Blessing of the Animals: True Stories of Ginny, the Dog Who Rescues Cats.* HarperPerennial, 1997.

Hempel, Amy and Jim Shepard, editors. *Unleashed: Poems by Writers' Dogs.* Crown Publishers, 1995.

Hess, Elizabeth. *Lost and Found: Dogs, Cats, and Everyday Heroes at a Country Animal Shelter.* Harcourt Brace and Company, 1998.

Kilcommons, Brian, and Sarah Wilson. *Childproofing Your Dog: A Complete Guide to Preparing Your Dog for the Children in Your Life.* Warner Books, 1994.

Lingenfelter, Mike and David Frei. *The Angel by My Side.* Hay House, 2002.

Mayle, Peter. *A Dog's Life.* Vintage Books, 1996.

McConnell, Patricia B., Ph.D. *The Other End of the Leash.* Ballantine Books, 2002.

Pryor, Karen. *Don't Shoot the Dog: The New Art of Teaching and Training.* Bantam Doubleday Dell Publishing, 1999.

The Bark Magazine, 2810 Eighth Street, Berkeley, CA 94710; www.thebark.com.

Welsh, Mark. *Sweetie: From the Gutter to the Runway, Tantalizing Tips From a Furry Fashionista.* Warner Books, 2001.

—— *Sweetie Says: I Never Met A Man I Didn't Lick: An Alphabet of Love.* Stewart, Tabori and Chang, 2002.